Los Angeles Angels 2020

A Baseball Companion

Edited by R.J. Anderson, Craig Goldstein and Bret Sayre

Baseball Prospectus

Craig Brown, Steven Goldman and David Pease, Consultant Editors
Robert Au, Harry Pavlidis and Amy Pircher, Statistics Editors

Copyright © 2020 by DIY Baseball, LLC.
All rights reserved

This book or any part thereof may not be reproduced or transmitted in any form or by any means, electronic or mechanical, including photocopying, recording, or by any information storage and retrieval system, without permission in writing from the publisher.

Limit of Liability/Disclaimer of Warranty: While the publisher and the author have used their best efforts in preparing this book, they make no representations or warranties with respect to the accuracy or completeness of the contents of this book and specifically disclaim any implied warranties of merchantability or fitness for a particular purpose. No warranty may be created or extended by sales representatives or written sales materials. The advice and strategies contained herein may not be suitable for your situation. You should consult with a professional where appropriate. Neither the publisher nor the author shall be liable for any loss of profit or any other commercial damages, including but not limited to special, incidental, consequential, or other damages.

Library of Congress Cataloging-in-Publication Data:
paperback
ISBN-13: 978-1-949332-78-0

Project Credits
Cover Design: Michael Byzewski at Aesthetic Apparatus
Interior Design and Production: Jeff Pease, Dave Pease
Layout: Jeff Pease, Dave Pease

Baseball icon courtesy of Uberux, from https://www.shareicon.net/author/uberux

Ballpark diagram courtesy of Lou Spirito/THIRTY81 Project, https://thirty81project.com/

Manufactured in the United States of America
10 9 8 7 6 5 4 3 2 1

Table of Contents

Statistical Introduction v

Part 1: Team Analysis

Los Angeles Angels: Where Are You Going, Where Have You Been? 3
   Colby Wilson, Jeffrey Paternostro and Matthew Trueblood

Performance Graphs 7

2019 Team Performance 8

2020 Team Projections 9

Team Personnel 10

Angel Stadium Stats 11

Angels Team Analysis 13

Part 2: Player Analysis

Angels Player Analysis 18

Angels Prospects 107

Part 3: Featured Articles

The Baseball Is Juiced (Again) 123
   Robert Arthur

The Moral Hazard of Playing It Safe 127
   Craig Goldstein

Index of Names 133

Statistical Introduction

Sports are, fundamentally, a blend of athletic endeavor and storytelling. Baseball, like any other sport, tells its stories in so many ways: in the arc of a game from the stands or a season from the box scores, in photos, or even in numbers. At Baseball Prospectus, we understand that statistics don't replace observation or any of baseball's stories, but complement everything else that makes the game so much fun.

What stats help us with is with patterns and precision, variance and value. This book can help you learn things you may not see from watching a game or hundred, whether it's the path of a career over time or the breadth of the entire MLB. We'd also never ask you to choose between our numbers and the experience of viewing a game from the cheap seats or the comfort of your home; our publication combines running the numbers with observations and wisdom from some of the brightest minds we can find. But if you *do* want to learn more about the numbers beyond what's on the backs of player jerseys, let us help explain.

Offense

We've revised our methodology for determining batting value. Long-time readers of the book will notice that we've retired True Average in favor of a new metric: Deserved Runs Created Plus (DRC+). Developed by Jonathan Judge and our stats team, this statistic measures everything a player does at the plate–reaching base, hitting for power, making outs, and moving runners over–and puts it on a scale where 100 equals league-average performance. A DRC+ of 150 is terrific, a DRC+ of 100 is average and a DRC+ of 75 means you better be an excellent defender.

DRC+ also does a better job than any of our previous metrics in taking contextual factors into account. The model adjusts for how the park affects performance, but also for things like the talent of the opposing pitcher, value of different types of batted-ball events, league, temperature and other factors. It's able to describe a player's expected offensive contribution than any other statistic we've found over the years, and also does a better job of predicting future performance as well.

There's a lot more to DRC+'s story, and you can read all about it in greater depth near the end of this book.

The other aspect of run-scoring is baserunning, which we quantify using Baserunning Runs. BRR not only records the value of stolen bases (or getting caught in the act), but also accounts for all the stuff that doesn't show up on the back of a baseball card: a runner's ability to go first to third on a single, or advance on a fly ball.

Defense

Where offensive value is *relatively* easy to identify and understand, defensive value is...not. Over the past dozen years, the sabermetric community has focused mostly on stats based on zone data: a real-live human person records the type of batted ball and estimated landing location, and models are created that give expected outs. From there, you can compare fielders' actual outs to those expected ones. Simple, right?

Unfortunately, zone data has two major issues. First, zone data is recorded by commercial data providers who keep the raw data private unless you pay for it. (All the statistics we build in this book and on our website use public data as inputs.) That hurts our ability to test assumptions or duplicate results. Second, over the years it has become apparent that there's quite a bit of "noise" in zone-based fielding analysis. Sometimes the conclusions drawn from zone data don't hold up to scrutiny, and sometimes the different data provided by different providers don't look anything alike, giving wildly different results. Sometimes the hard-working professional stringers or scorers might unknowingly inflict unconscious bias into the mix: for example good fielders will often be credited with more expected outs despite the data, and ballparks with high press boxes tend to score more line drives than ones with a lower press box.

Enter our Fielding Runs Above Average (FRAA). For most positions, FRAA is built from play-by-play data, which allows us to avoid the subjectivity found in many other fielding metrics. The idea is this: count how many fielding plays are made by a given player and compare that to expected plays for an average fielder at their position (based on pitcher ground ball tendencies and batter handedness). Then we adjust for park and base-out situations.

When it comes to catchers, our methodology is a little different thanks to the laundry list of responsibilities they're tasked with beyond just, well, catching and throwing the ball. By now you've probably heard about "framing" or the art of making umpires more likely to call balls outside the strike zone for strikes. To put this into one tidy number, we incorporate pitch tracking data (for the years it exists) and adjust for important factors like pitcher, umpire, batter and home-field advantage using a mixed-model approach. This grants us a number for how many strikes the catcher is personally adding to (or subtracting from) his pitchers' performance...which we then convert to runs added or lost using linear weights.

Framing is one of the biggest parts of determining catcher value, but we also take into account blocking balls from going past, whether a scorer deems it a passed ball or a wild pitch. We use a similar approach—one that really benefits from the pitch tracking data that tells us what ends up in the dirt and what doesn't. We also include a catcher's ability to prevent stolen bases and how well they field balls in play, and *finally* we come up with our FRAA for catchers.

Pitching

Both pitching and fielding make up the half of baseball that isn't run scoring: run prevention. Separating pitching from fielding is a tough task, and most recent pitching analysis has branched off from Voros McCracken's famous (and controversial) statement, "There is little if any difference among major-league pitchers in their ability to prevent hits on balls hit in the field of play." The research of the analytic community has validated this to some extent, and there are a host of "defense-independent" pitching measures that have been developed to try and extract the effect of the defense behind a hurler from the pitcher's work.

Our solution to this quandary is Deserved Run Average (DRA), our core pitching metric. DRA looks like earned run average (ERA), the tried-and-true pitching stat you've seen on every baseball broadcast or box score from the past century, but it's very different. To start, DRA takes an event-by-event look at what the pitchers does, and adjusts the value of that event based on different environmental factors like park, batter, catcher, umpire, base-out situation, run differential, inning, defense, home field advantage, pitcher role and temperature. That mixed model gives us a pitcher's expected contribution, similar to what we do for our DRC+ model for hitters and FRAA model for catchers. (Oh, and we also consider the pitcher's effect on basestealing and on balls getting past the catcher.)

It's important to note that DRA is set to the scale of runs allowed per nine innings (RA9) instead of ERA, which makes DRA's scale slightly higher than ERA's. The reason for this is because ERA tends to overrate three types of pitchers:

1. Pitchers who play in parks where scorers hand out more errors. Official scorers differ significantly in the frequency at which they assign errors to fielders.
2. Ground-ball pitchers, because a substantial proportion of errors occur on groundballs.
3. Pitchers who aren't very good. Better pitchers often allow fewer unearned runs than bad pitchers, because good pitchers tend to find ways to get out of jams.

Los Angeles Angels 2020

Since the last time you picked up an edition of this book, we've also made a few minor changes to DRA to make it better. Recent research into "tunneling"—the act of throwing consecutive pitches that appear similar from a batter's point of view until after the swing decision point–data has given us a new contextual factor to account for in DRA: plate distance. This refers to the distance between successive pitches as they approach the plate, and while it has a smaller effect than factors like velocity or whiff rate, it still can help explain pitcher strikeout rate in our model.

New Pitching Metrics for 2020

We're including a few "new" pitching metrics in the book for the 2020 edition, though unlike last year, these numbers may be a little bit more familiar to those of you who have spent some time investigating baseball statistics.

Fastball Percentage

Our fastball percentage (FB%) statistic measures how frequently a pitcher throws a pitch classified as a "fastball," measured as a percentage of overall pitches thrown. We qualify three types of fastballs:

1. The traditional four-seam fastball;
2. The two-seam fastball or sinker;
3. "Hard cutters," which are pitches that have the movement profile of a cut fastball and are used as the pitcher's primary offering or in place of a more traditional fastball.

For example, a pitcher with a FB% of 67 throws any combination of these three pitches about two-thirds of the time.

Whiff Rate

Everybody loves a swing and a miss, and whiff rate (WHF) measures how frequently pitchers induce a swinging strike. To calculate WHF, we add up all the pitches thrown that ended with a swinging strike, then divide that number by a pitcher's total pitches thrown. Most often, high whiff rates correlate with high strikeout rates (and overall effective pitcher performance).

Called Strike Probability

Called Strike Probability (CSP) is a number that represents the likelihood that all of a pitcher's pitches will be called a strike while controlling for location, pitcher and batter handedness, umpire and count. Here's how it works: on each pitch, our model determines how many times (out of 100) that a similar pitch was called for a strike given those factors mentioned above, and when normalized for each batter's strike zone. Then we average the CSP for all pitches thrown by a pitcher in a season, and that gives us the yearly CSP percentage you see in the stats boxes.

As you might imagine, pitchers with a higher CSP are more likely to work in the zone, where pitchers with a lower CSP are likely locating their pitches outside the normal strike zone, for better or for worse.

Projections

Many of you aren't turning to this book just for a look at what a player has done, but for a look at what a player is going to do: the PECOTA projections. PECOTA, initially developed by Nate Silver (who has moved on to greater fame as a political analyst), consists of three parts:

1. Major-league equivalencies, which use minor-league statistics to project how a player will perform in the major leagues;
2. Baseline forecasts, which use weighted averages and regression to the mean to estimate a player's current true talent level; and
3. Aging curves, which uses the career paths of comparable players to estimate how a player's statistics are likely to change over time.

With all those important things covered, let's take a look at what's in the book this year.

Team Prospectus

Most of this book is composed of team chapters, with one for each of the 30 major-league franchises. On the first page of each chapter, you'll see a box that contains some of the key statistics for each team as well as a very inviting stadium diagram. (You can see an example of this for the Milwaukee Brewers on this very page!)

We start with the team name, their unadjusted 2019 win-loss record, and their divisional ranking. Beneath that are a host of other team statistics. **Pythag** presents an adjusted 2019 winning percentage, calculated by taking runs scored per game (**RS/G**) and runs allowed per game (**RA/G**) for the team, and running them through a version of Bill James' Pythagorean formula that was refined and improved by David Smyth and Brandon Heipp. (The formula is called "Pythagenpat," which is equally fun to type and to say.)

Next up is **DRC+**, described earlier, to indicate the overall hitting ability of the team either above or below league-average. Run prevention on the pitching side is covered by **DRA** (also mentioned earlier) and another metric: Fielding Independent Pitching (**FIP**), which calculates another ERA-like statistic based on strikeouts, walks, and home runs recorded. Defensive Efficiency Rating (**DER**) tells us the percentage of balls in play turned into outs for the team, and is a quick fielding shorthand that rounds out run prevention.

After that, we have several measures related to roster composition, as opposed to on-field performance. **B-Age** and **P-Age** tell us the average age of a team's batters and pitchers, respectively. **Salary** is the combined team payroll for all on-field players, and Doug Pappas' Marginal Dollars per Marginal Win (**M$/MW**) tells us how much money a team spent to earn production above replacement level.

Ending this batch of statistics is the number of disabled list days a team had over the season (**IL Days**) and the amount of salary paid to players on the disabled list (**$ on IL**); this final number is expressed as a percentage of total payroll.

Next to each of these stats, we've listed each team's MLB rank in that category from first to 30th. In this, first always indicates a positive outcome and 30th a negative outcome, except in the case of salary—first is highest.

After the franchise statistics, we share a few items about the team's home ballpark. There's the aforementioned diagram of the park's dimensions (including distances to the outfield wall), a graphic showing the height of the wall from the left-field pole to the right-field pole, and a table showing three-year park factors for the stadium. The park factors are displayed as indexes where 100 is average, 110 means that the park inflates the statistic in question by 10 percent, and 90 means that the park deflates the statistic in question by 10 percent.

On the second page of each team chapter, you'll find three graphs. The first is the **2019 Hit List Ranking**. This shows our Hit List Rank for the team on each day of the 2019 season and is intended to give you a picture of the ups and downs of the team's season. Hit List Rank measures overall team performance and drives the Hit List Power Rankings at the baseballprospectus.com website.

The second graph is **Committed Payroll** and helps you see how the team's payroll has compared to the MLB and divisional average payrolls over time. Payroll figures are current as of January 1, 2020; with so many free agents still unsigned as of this writing, the final 2020 figure will likely be significantly different for many teams. (In the meantime, you can always find the most current data at Baseball Prospectus' Cot's Baseball Contracts page.)

The third graph is **Farm System Ranking** and displays how the Baseball Prospectus prospect team has ranked the organization's farm system since 2007.

After the graphs, we have a **Personnel** section that lists many of the important decision-makers and upper-level field and operations staff members for the franchise, as well as any former Baseball Prospectus staff members who are currently part of the organization. (In very rare circumstances, someone might be on both lists!)

Juan Soto LF
Born: 10/25/98 Age: 21 Bats: L Throws: L
Height: 6'1" Weight: 185 Origin: International Free Agent, 2015

YEAR	TEAM	LVL	AGE	PA	R	2B	3B	HR	RBI	BB	K	SB	CS	AVG/OBP/SLG
2017	NAT	RK	18	27	3	1	1	0	4	2	1	0	0	.320/.370/.440
2017	HAG	A	18	96	15	5	0	3	14	10	8	1	2	.360/.427/.523
2018	HAG	A	19	74	12	5	3	5	24	14	13	2	0	.373/.486/.814
2018	POT	A+	19	73	17	3	1	7	18	11	8	0	1	.371/.466/.790
2018	HAR	AA	19	35	4	2	0	2	10	4	7	1	0	.323/.400/.581
2018	WAS	MLB	19	494	77	25	1	22	70	79	99	5	2	.292/.406/.517
2019	WAS	MLB	20	659	110	32	5	34	110	108	132	12	1	.282/.401/.548
2020	WAS	MLB	21	630	92	30	3	35	102	85	123	5	2	.284/.382/.543

Comparables: Ronald Acuña Jr., Mike Trout, Tony Conigliaro

YEAR	TEAM	LVL	AGE	PA	DRC+	VORP	BABIP	BRR	FRAA	WARP
2017	NAT	RK	18	27	135	1.5	.333	0.0	RF(9): -1.1	0.0
2017	HAG	A	18	96	181	8.0	.373	1.0	RF(19): -1.9, LF(2): -0.3	0.9
2018	HAG	A	19	74	222	14.5	.405	0.3	RF(14): 1.1, CF(2): 0.2	1.2
2018	POT	A+	19	73	260	15.4	.340	1.4	RF(14): 1.0, LF(1): 0.0	1.6
2018	HAR	AA	19	35	113	3.6	.364	0.0	LF(4): 0.6, RF(4): -0.5	0.1
2018	WAS	MLB	19	494	125	40.5	.338	-0.5	LF(114): 2.7	3.0
2019	WAS	MLB	20	659	136	49.0	.312	1.4	LF(150): -0.8	4.9
2020	WAS	MLB	21	630	133	43.6	.310	-0.1	LF 3	4.8

Position Players

After all that information and a thoughtful bylined essay covering each team, we present our player comments. These are also bylined, but due to frequent franchise shifts during the offseason, our bylines are more a rough guide than a perfect accounting of who wrote what.

Each player is listed with the major-league team that employed him as of early January 2020. If a player changed teams after that point via free agency, trade, or any other method, you'll be able to find them in the chapter for their previous squad.

As an example, take a look at the player comment for Nationals outfielder Juan Soto: the stat block that accompanies his written comment is at the top of this page. First we cover biographical information (age is as of June 30, 2020) before moving onto the stats themselves. Our statistic columns include standard identifying information like **YEAR**, **TEAM**, **LVL** (level of affiliated play) and **AGE** before getting into the numbers. Next, we provide raw, untranslated numbers like you might find on the back of your dad's baseball cards: **PA** (plate appearances), **R** (runs), **2B** (doubles), **3B** (triples), **HR** (home runs), **RBI** (runs batted in), **BB** (walks), **K** (strikeouts), **SB** (stolen bases) and **CS** (caught stealing).

Los Angeles Angels 2020

Next, we have unadjusted "slash" statistics: **AVG** (batting average), **OBP** (on-base percentage) and **SLG** (slugging percentage). Following the slash line is **DRC+** (Deserved Runs Created Plus), which we described earlier as total offensive expected contribution compared to the league average.

One of our oldest active metrics, **VORP** (Value Over Replacement Player), considers offensive production, position and plate appearances. In essence, it is the number of runs contributed beyond what a replacement-level player at the same position would contribute if given the same percentage of team plate appearances. VORP does not consider the quality of a player's defense.

BABIP (batting average on balls in play) tells us how often a ball in play fell for a hit, and can help us identify whether a batter may have been lucky or not...but note that high BABIPs also tend to follow the great hitters of our time, as well as speedy singles hitters who put the ball on the ground.

The next item is **BRR** (Baserunning Runs), which covers all of a player's baserunning accomplishments including (but not limited to) swiped bags and failed attempts. Next is **FRAA** (Fielding Runs Above Average), which also includes the number of games previously played at each position noted in parentheses. Multi-position players have only their two most frequent positions listed here, but their total FRAA number reflects all positions played.

Our last column here is **WARP** (Wins Above Replacement Player). WARP estimates the total value of a player, which means for hitters it takes into account hitting runs above average (calculated using the DRC+ model), BRR and FRAA. Then, it makes an adjustment for positions played and gives the player a credit for plate appearances based upon the difference between "replacement level"—which is derived from the quality of players added to a team's roster after the start of the season–and the league average.

The final line just below the stats box is **PECOTA** data, which is discussed further in a following section.

Catchers

Catchers are a special breed, and thus they have earned their own separate box which displays some of the defensive metrics that we've built just for them. As an example, let's check out J.T. Realmuto.

The **YEAR** and **TEAM** columns match what you'd find in the other stat box. **P. COUNT** indicates the number of pitches thrown while the catcher was behind the plate, including swinging strikes, fouls and balls in play. **FRM RUNS** is the total run value the catcher provided (or cost) his team by influencing the umpire to call strikes where other catchers did not. **BLK RUNS** expresses the total run value above or below average for the catcher's ability to prevent wild pitches and passed balls. **THRW RUNS** is calculated using a similar model as the previous two statistics, and it measures a catcher's ability to throw out basestealers but also to dissuade them from testing his arm in the first place. It takes into account factors like the pitcher (including his delivery and pickoff move) and baserunner (who could be as fast as Billy Hamilton or as slow as Yonder Alonso). **TOT RUNS** is the sum of all of the previous three statistics.

Justin Verlander   RHP
Born: 02/20/83   Age: 37   Bats: R   Throws: R
Height: 6'5"   Weight: 225   Origin: Round 1, 2004 Draft (#2 overall)

YEAR	TEAM	LVL	AGE	W	L	SV	G	GS	IP	H	HR	BB/9	K/9	K	GB%	BABIP
2017	DET	MLB	34	10	8	0	28	28	172	153	23	3.5	9.2	176	34%	.283
2017	HOU	MLB	34	5	0	0	5	5	34	17	4	1.3	11.4	43	32%	.194
2018	HOU	MLB	35	16	9	0	34	34	214	156	28	1.6	12.2	290	31%	.272
2019	HOU	MLB	36	21	6	0	34	34	223	137	36	1.7	12.1	300	36%	.219
2020	HOU	MLB	37	15	6	0	29	29	184	138	28	2.3	12.1	248	35%	.274

Comparables: Zack Greinke, A.J. Burnett, Aníbal Sánchez

YEAR	TEAM	LVL	AGE	WHIP	ERA	DRA	WARP	MPH	FB%	WHF	CSP
2017	DET	MLB	34	1.28	3.82	4.03	3.0	97.7	58	11	47.8
2017	HOU	MLB	34	0.65	1.06	3.08	0.9	97.5	59.6	15.1	49.9
2018	HOU	MLB	35	0.90	2.52	2.33	7.3	97.5	61.2	16.2	51.6
2019	HOU	MLB	36	0.80	2.58	2.51	7.9	96.8	49.9	17.5	48.3
2020	HOU	MLB	37	1.01	2.75	2.95	5.3	95.8	54.6	15.1	48.2

Pitchers

Let's give our pitchers a turn, using 2019 AL Cy Young winner Justin Verlander as our example. Take a look at his stat block: the first line and the **YEAR**, **TEAM**, **LVL** and **AGE** columns are the same as in the position player example earlier.

Here too, we have a series of columns that display raw, unadjusted statistics compiled by the pitcher over the course of a season: **W** (wins), **L** (losses), **SV** (saves), **G** (games pitched), **GS** (games started), **IP** (innings pitched), **H** (hits allowed) and **HR** (home runs allowed). Next we have two statistics that are rates: **BB/9** (walks per nine innings) and **K/9** (strikeouts per nine innings), before returning to the unadjusted K (strikeouts).

Next up is **GB%** (ground ball percentage), which is the percentage of all batted balls that were hit on the ground, including both outs and hits. Remember, this is based on observational data and subject to human error, so please approach this with a healthy dose of skepticism.

BABIP (batting average on balls in play) is calculated using the same methodology as it is for position players, but it often tells us more about a pitcher than it does a hitter. With pitchers, a high BABIP is often due to poor defense or bad luck, and can often be an indicator of potential rebound, and a low BABIP may be cause to expect performance regression. (A typical league-average BABIP is close to .290-.300.)

Los Angeles Angels 2020

The metrics **WHIP** (walks plus hits per inning pitched) and **ERA** (earned run average) are old standbys: WHIP measures walks and hits allowed on a per-inning basis, while ERA measures earned runs on a nine-inning basis. Neither of these stats are translated or adjusted.

DRA (Deserved Run Average) was described at length earlier, and measures how many runs the pitcher "deserved" to allow per nine innings. Please note that since we lack all the data points that would make for a "real" DRA for minor-league events, the DRA displayed for minor league partial-seasons is based off of different data. (That data is a modified version of our cFIP metric, which you can find more information about on our website.)

Just like with hitters, **WARP** (Wins Above Replacement Player) is a total value metric that puts pitchers of all stripes on the same scale as position players. We use DRA as the primary input for our calculation of WARP. You might notice that relief pitchers (due to their limited innings) may have a lower WARP than you were expecting or than you might see in other WARP-like metrics. WARP does not take leverage into account, just the actions a pitcher performs and the expected value of those actions...which ends up judging high-leverage relief pitchers differently than you might imagine given their prestige and market value.

MPH gives you the pitcher's 95th percentile velocity for the noted season, in order to give you an idea of what the *peak* fastball velocity a pitcher possesses. Since this comes from our pitch-tracking data, it is not publicly available for minor-league pitchers.

Finally, we display the three new pitching metrics we described earlier. **FB%** (fastball percentage) gives you the percentage of fastballs thrown out of all pitches. **WHF** (whiff rate) tells you the percentage of swinging strikes induced out of all pitches. **CSP** (called strike probability) expresses the likelihood of all pitches thrown to result in a called strike, after controlling for factors like handedness, umpire, pitch type, count and location.

PECOTA

All players have PECOTA projections for 2020, as well as a set of other numbers that describe the performance of comparable players according to PECOTA. All projections for 2020 are for the player at the date we went to press in early January and are projected into the league and park context as indicated by the team abbreviation. (Note that players at very low levels of the minors are too unpredictable to assess using these numbers.) All PECOTA projected statistics represent a player's projected major-league performance.

Below the projections are the player's three highest-scoring comparable players as determined by PECOTA. All comparables represent a snapshot of how the listed player was performing at the same age as the current player, so if a

23-year-old pitcher is compared to Bartolo Colón, he's actually being compared to a 23-year-old Colón, not the version that pitched for the Rangers in 2018, nor to Colón's career as a whole.

A few points about pitcher projections. First, we aren't yet projecting peak velocity, so that column will be blank in the PECOTA lines. Second, projecting DRA is trickier than evaluating past performance, because it is unclear how deserving each pitcher will be of his anticipated outcomes. However, we know that another DRA-related statistic–contextual FIP or cFIP–estimates future run scoring very well. So for PECOTA, the projected DRA figures you see are based on the past cFIPs generated by the pitcher and comparable players over time, along with the other factors described above.

Lineouts

In each chapter's Lineouts section, you'll find abbreviated text comments, as well as all the same information you'd find in our full player comments. The only difference is that we limit the stats boxes in this section to only including the 2019 information for each player.

Managers

After all those wonderful team chapters, we've got statistics for each big-league manager, all of whom are organized by alphabetical order. Here you'll find a block including an extraordinary amount of information collected from each manager's entire career. For more information on the acronyms and what they mean, please visit the Glossary at www.baseballprospectus.com.

There is one important metric that we'd like to call attention to, and you'll find it next to each manager's name: **wRM+** (weighted reliever management plus). Developed by Rob Arthur and Rian Watt, wRM+ investigates how good a manager is at using their best relievers during the moments of highest leverage, using both our proprietary DRA metric as well as Leverage Index. wRM+ is scaled to a league average of 100, and a wRM+ of 105 indicates that relievers were used approximately five percent "better" than average. On the other hand, a wRM+ of 95 would tell us the team used its relievers five percent "worse" than the average team.

While wRM+ does not have an extremely strong correlation with a manager, it is statistically significant; this means that a manager is not *entirely* responsible for a team's wRM+, but does have some effect on that number.

PECOTA Leaderboards

If you're familiar with PECOTA, then you'll have noticed that the projection system often appears bullish on players coming off a bad year and bearish on players coming off a good year. (This is because the system weights several previous seasons, not just the most recent one.) In addition, we publish the 50th

Los Angeles Angels 2020

percentile projections for each player–which is smack in the middle of the range of projected production—which tends to mean PECOTA stat lines don't often have extreme results like 40 home runs or 250 strikeouts in a given season. In essence, PECOTA doesn't project very many extreme seasons.

At the end of the book, we've ranked the top players at each position based on their PECOTA projections. This might help you visualize just how a given player's projection compares to that of their peers, so that even if a dramatic stat line isn't projected, you can still imagine how they stack up against the rest of the league.

Part 1: Team Analysis

Los Angeles Angels: Where Are You Going, Where Have You Been?

Colby Wilson, Jeffrey Paternostro and Matthew Trueblood

2019: What Went Right
The short answer is, "Mike Trout." His power numbers continue to steadily improve. He may not be a 40-40 threat anymore, but he's among the smartest baserunners in the league. He's not a human highlight reel, but he's sure-handed. Not only does his game not have holes, the weaknesses feel laughably weak, as though we're making the argument more because we should than because we believe it.

But it wasn't *just* Trout! It was *mostly* just Trout. Shohei Ohtani proved himself more than capable of being an everyday part of the lineup when his arm is hopefully mended. An actual piece in Brian Goodwin may have been dropped into the Angels' lap when the Royals DFA'd him to keep Lucas Duda; always streaky, Goodwin opened the season on a tear and then spent a couple of months making outs, rebounded again, then collapsed in September. The highs outweighed the lows, especially for a team that has frequently struggled to bracket Trout with productive players in one or both corners.

The Tommy La Stella/Andrelton Simmons left side of the infield was productive, at least when both or either were healthy enough to be on the field. Sophomore David Fletcher played well enough in his first full major league season to suggest he could be a useful regular on both sides of the ball, although he'll have to keep his batting average up to compensate for his lack of pop. One of the harder players in the AL to strike out, he's a lucky balls-in-play season away from doing just that. Kole Calhoun rebounded from a miserable 2018 and set a career high in home runs in his last season in Halos togs.

2019: What Went Wrong

The pitching was bad, but that seems beside the point given what the staff (and the team) had to endure in 2019. To discuss Tyler Skaggs' untimely, tragic death in baseball terms would be callous, tone-deaf, monstrous. The Angels lost a friend, a brother, a person. Whatever successes or failures they may have had in 2019, that has to be taken as part of the equation.

As a whole, the pitching staff—from rotation to bullpen—did not enjoy its best year in 2019. The no-hitter—the Taylor Cole/Félix Peña combined no-hitter in the Angels' first home game since Skaggs' passing, on a night when his mother threw out the first pitch—was the single most profound, uplifting moment baseball had to offer in 2019. That it was authored by a bottom-five team in WAR, FIP, DRA and most other acronyms you'd care to find won't change that. In a game that feels increasingly less in touch with its own humanity, this erstwhile child's game provided a moment of sublimity. To ask for anything more, to ask for *one thing more*, of the Angels' 2019 season, like a playoff appearance or even one more win, would be to shortchange a profound and lasting moment of collective consolation for a transient and ultimately hollow triumph.

There were many injuries. In addition, some of the team's gambles—Jonathan Lucroy, Cody Allen, Peter Bourjos, Matt Harvey—were terrible. It's always understandable when teams hope to coax the last good season or two out of a veteran. It's odd when a team in the Los Angeles market with a number of aging or prime-of-their-career greats goes that route to the extent the Angels have.
—*Colby Wilson*

Prospect Outlook

Jo Adell. What, you were expecting Patrick Sandoval or Matt Thaiss? Adell missed the first two months of the season after a nasty looking leg injury in spring training, but he appeared no worse for wear over the balance of the 2019 season. Adell offers true impact talent standing on either side of Trout on the outfield grass. He has the foot-speed and outfield instincts to play center, but will probably have to settle for being plus-or-better in a corner. There is 7 hit/7 power potential in the bat. He's one of the best prospects in baseball and is just about ready for action in Anaheim.

The rest of the system had an uneven 2019. The young impact talent is still young and still carries impact potential, but we will have to wait another year for the outfielders **Jordyn Adams**, **Trent Deveaux**, or **D'Shawn Knowles** breakout. **Jahmai Jones** continued to struggle with the bat after his transition to second base. OF **Brandon Marsh** more or less held serve, but still hasn't seen his above-average raw power translate into minor league games. The Angels' system is still loads of fun, but it's more fun than great at the moment. —*Jeffrey Paternostro*

2020 Outlook

It should still count as a moderate disappointment for Angels fans that the team went into the winter with so much money to spend and such a clear need, but emerged without a new frontline starting pitcher. The only reason that disappointment should be moderate, and not extreme, is that the Angels nailed everything else this winter.

Hiring Joe Maddon to manage was a great start. Maddon may not be the visionary or the top-tier tactician he was a decade ago, but he still keeps a clubhouse loose and enthusiastic, and his arrival is always a signal of a team's intention to win. Anthony Rendon, of course, is more important, because he makes the Angels much better on both sides of the runs ledger, and because he adds a second cornerstone around which to build, but bringing Maddon back to where he spent the first two decades of his coaching career was an excellent first step.

Though no superstar, Jason Castro raises the projection for catcher production by showing up in Anaheim nearly as much as Yasmani Grandal did by signing with the White Sox. The position was a black hole for the Angels last year (.221/.293/.344), and now, they have a competent, lefty-hitting veteran backstop, at a lowish price. Arte Moreno authorized big spending, but made Billy Eppler demonstrate his good faith, and the latter went about that well. By not picking up Calhoun's club option, Eppler opened up right field for Adell and saved money he was able to put toward the rotation. Dylan Bundy and Julio Teheran would be a much more exciting pair of additions if it were five years ago, but each is a competent big-league starter with stability to offer. —*Matthew Trueblood*

Performance Graphs

2019 Hit List Ranking

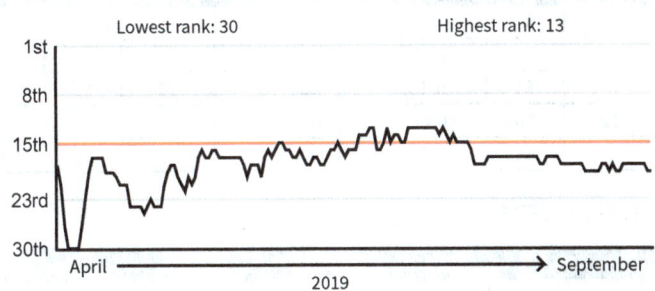

Committed Payroll (in millions)

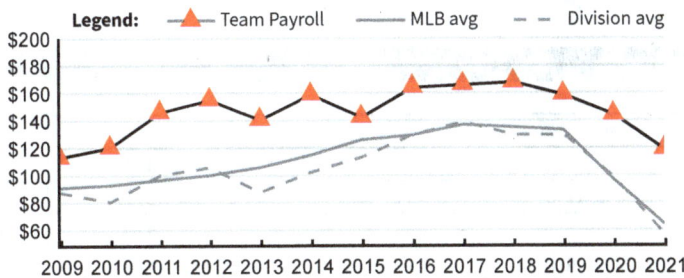

Farm System Ranking

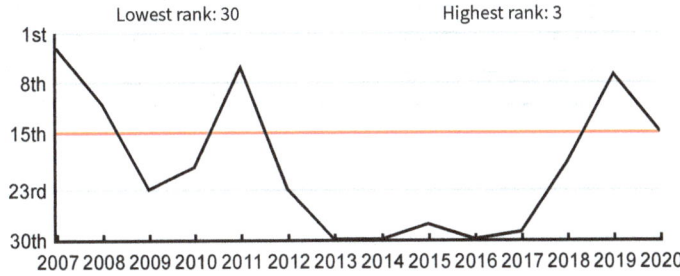

2019 Team Performance

ACTUAL STANDINGS

Team	W	L	Pct
HOU	107	55	0.660
OAK	97	65	0.599
TEX	78	84	0.481
LAA	**72**	**90**	**0.444**
SEA	68	94	0.420

THIRD-ORDER STANDINGS

Team	W	L	Pct
HOU	117	45	0.719
OAK	95	67	0.584
LAA	**73**	**89**	**0.453**
SEA	72	90	0.444
TEX	71	91	0.437

TOP HITTERS

Player	WARP
Mike Trout	8.9
Kole Calhoun	3.1
David Fletcher	2.5

TOP PITCHERS

Player	WARP
Félix Peña	1.4
Ty Buttrey	1.4
Hansel Robles	1.3

VITAL STATISTICS

Statistic Name	Value	Rank
Pythagenpat	.441	19th
Runs Scored per Game	4.75	15th
Runs Allowed per Game	5.36	23rd
Deserved Runs Created Plus	101	8th
Deserved Run Average	5.63	26th
Fielding Independent Pitching	5.07	28th
Defensive Efficiency Rating	.710	8th
Batter Age	28.8	24th
Pitcher Age	26.9	4th
Salary	$158.9M	8th
Marginal $ per Marginal Win	$6.2M	7th
Injured List Days	1603	27th
$ on IL	26%	25th

2020 Team Projections

PROJECTED STANDINGS

Team	W	L	Pct	+/-
HOU	98.3	63.7	0.607	-9
LAA	**86.8**	**75.2**	**0.536**	**15**
OAK	84.6	77.4	0.522	-12
TEX	73.0	89.0	0.451	-5
SEA	66.0	96.0	0.407	-2

TOP PROJECTED HITTERS

Player	WARP
Mike Trout	8.8
Anthony Rendon	3.7
Justin Upton	3.6

TOP PROJECTED PITCHERS

Player	WARP
Griffin Canning	1.5
Andrew Heaney	1.4
Julio Teheran	1.2

FARM SYSTEM REPORT

Top Prospect	Number of Top 101 Prospects
Jo Adell, #2	4

KEY DEDUCTIONS

Player	WARP
Kole Calhoun	1.1
Zack Cozart	0.1
Adalberto Mejía	0.1
Luis García	0.0
Jake Jewell	-0.1
Kean Wong	-0.2
Luis Madero	-0.2

KEY ADDITIONS

Player	WARP
Anthony Rendon	3.7
Jason Castro	1.5
Julio Teheran	1.2
Matt Andriese	0.7
Dylan Bundy	0.5
José Quijada	0.1
Jahmai Jones	0.0
Kyle Keller	0.0
Hector Yan	-0.1
Parker Markel	-0.2

Team Personnel

General Manager
Billy Eppler

Assistant General Manager
Steve Martone

Assistant General Manager
Jonathan Strangio

Director, Baseball Operations
Andrew Ball

Manager
Joe Maddon

Angel Stadium Stats

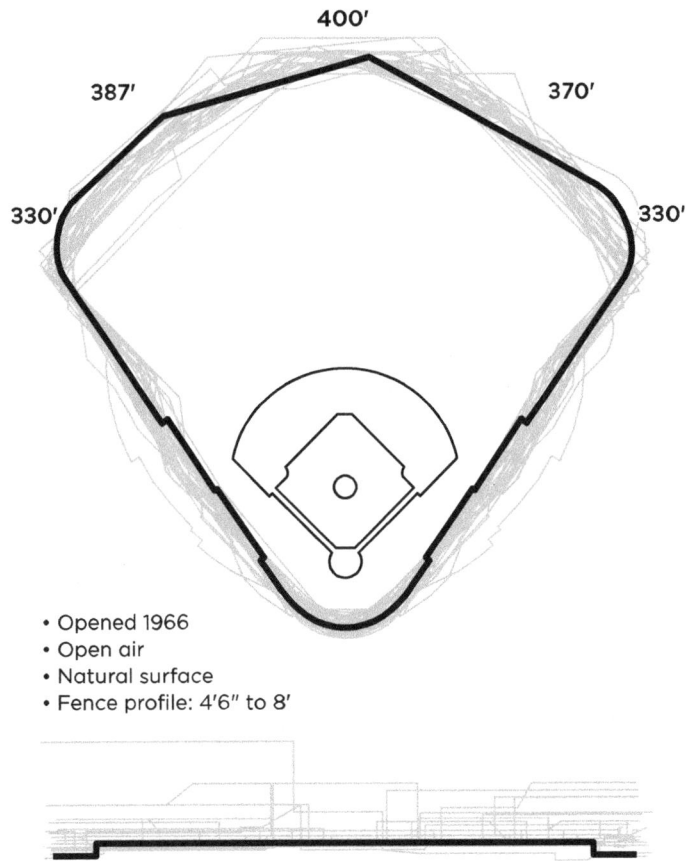

- Opened 1966
- Open air
- Natural surface
- Fence profile: 4'6" to 8'

Three-Year Park Factors

Runs	Runs/RH	Runs/LH	HR/RH	HR/LH
98	98	100	101	107

Angels Team Analysis

If you were to wander the streets of some major city, claiming that Mike Trout played for the Seattle Pilots, how many people would believe it? It's not as outlandish a question as it might seem—Trout's abilities demand a generational legacy of his play, a legend in the same mold as Mantle or Williams. If baseball is still a going concern in decades, Trout's story will be an integral part of it. His team though? Not so much. The greatness of Trout underlines the core paradox of his team: No one cares about the Los Angeles Angels, and yet everyone watches them.

Erstwhile Angels manager Mike Scioscia was well-known for his box of sayings, with his most commonly used mantra at the end of his reign perhaps being "turn the page." The Angels have done lots of page-turning of late, so much that their second season post-Scioscia brings another new manager. Last season was the Angels' worst campaign of the century, whether mounted from Los Angeles, Anaheim or Los Angeles of Anaheim. The last time the Angels were worse than the 72-90 was 1999, when only a strong finish (19-10) under interim manager Joe Maddon brought them to 71 wins. The team has long been searching, increasingly frantically, for its next chapter, something worth remembering.

It's not meant pejoratively, but more as a matter of fact: Despite the presence of a true contender for baseball's "best ever" crown, continued futility has turned the team into an afterthought. Joke does not seem the harshest descriptor, given the prevalence of the "wasting Mike Trout" refrain that grows harder to deny each season the team is functionally eliminated by the trade deadline. The Angels have consciously courted the same media market as the Dodgers, who since 2013 have surpassed them by six division titles and 204 wins. While Commissioner Rob Manfred has criticized Trout for not cultivating his own legend, a much more obvious critique is of the failure of his organization to put talent around its homegrown superstar. The 2020 season is, as much as it is about winning, a challenge in relevance.

Things have to get better for the Angels, if almost by default, since they spent the latter half of the year eliminated from contention and embroiled in tragedy and scandal. The tragic death of Tyler Skaggs, and subsequent revelation of Angels employees with knowledge of and involvement in the pitcher's opioid use, tinged everything that followed: a deeply emotional combined no-hitter, a freefall sans Trout to end the season, the firing of Brad Ausmus and installation of former bench coach Joe Maddon.

Los Angeles Angels 2020

In spite of it all, some 3,019,012 people were reported as coming to see Trout & Co. The teams surrounding the Angels on the attendance list—the Cubs, Rockies and Red Sox—suggest a certain level of insularity from performance. The Angels' last game of the season was started by Dillon Peters. Brian Goodwin hit third! 34,693 arrived to bear witness, and were treated to a perfect encapsulation of their season: Peters failed to escape the fourth and the Angels never held the lead and were out of it by the seventh-inning stretch. For the 162nd time, the team showed up, the fans did too, but the positives ended there.

Last season was not the most injury-laden for Angels pitchers in recent memory, but, it might well have been the worst. Experiments with starters Matt Harvey and Trevor Cahill, and closer Cody Allen are better left as forgotten as the team's Disney phase, and their underperformance—plus the void left by Skaggs' passing—put a lot on rookie starters, and, more frequently, the bullpen. The Angels received a franchise record 761 2/3 relief innings, one of just four instances in league history where a team saw its bullpen rack up more frames than its rotation. None of the other entrants, the 2018-19 Rays and the 2019 Blue Jays, were known for playing a particularly alluring brand of baseball.

In contrast to the beleaguered pitchers, the Angels offense has long been fine. With Mike Trout consistently 75-plus percent above league average (and age-related decline hopefully years down the line), it'd take something truly putrid for the lineup as a whole to rest below. With Anthony Rendon likely hitting behind Trout most days, the ceiling is the league's best offense. The team has to lean on a lot of rebounds, however: No one's expecting Albert Pujols to be more than replacement-level at this point, but Shohei Ohtani, Andrelton Simmons and Justin Upton each struggled with injury and underperformance. The latter two sitting on the wrong side of 30 makes a return to form unassured. Top prospect Jo Adell waits in the wings, with space cleared for him by a declined Kole Calhoun option. It's unclear if he'll have to play the service-time waiting game. And, in any case, the underwhelming rookie season of Vladimir Guerrero Jr. gives a rejoinder against expecting every uber-prospect to perform immediately on the level of Ronald Acuña Jr.

It's clear Moreno wants the Angels to be more than an also-ran. The Rendon signing aligns with the Pujols and Josh Hamilton deals in more than its boundary-pushing AAV: While there were myriad factors that caused him to land in Southern California rather than Gerrit Cole and Stephen Strasburg, Rendon reaffirms a preference to spend on position players and their possibility for daily contributions, rather than the once-every-five-days model for starting pitchers. It's not that there's no logic there; the team's own track record of fragile starters underscores that, but the team's failure to make a big splash in the rotation puts a lot on a group reasonably described as Ohtani et al.

It's fair to argue that Rendon was the best player available in the offseason, but there are just as many reasons to think Angels fans have heard this story before. Rendon is coming off a 6.3 WARP season, and will be entering his age-30 season in 2020. Pujols recorded a 6.4 WARP campaign in his final year in St. Louis, and arrived in Anaheim for his age-31 season. Upton, meanwhile, was coming off a 4.9 WARP effort split between Detroit and Anaheim, before re-upping ahead of his age-30 season. Rendon, perhaps, combines the best of those two qualities, and therefore could be the best veteran teammate of Trout's tenure—but one can't blame the fanbase for feeling like Lucy is holding a football, saying this time it's different.

Meanwhile, Billy Eppler leaned hard into reliability for the rotation, ultimately winding up with a mostly durable group with shaky upside. If Andrew Heaney can put it all together in his walk year for a repeat of 2018, he's probably still a third starter. Ohtani is an aberration all his own, but a full healthy season would still represent a mutation of sorts for the flamethrower, entering his third year in the league. Julio Teherán and Dylan Bundy will probably help ensure the rotation again outstrips the bullpen in frames, if simultaneously pushing the group downwards in rate metrics. Collected together, it's hardly an intimidating list of names.

Here is the problem, however: The Angels are a team with little identity or attraction besides an archipelago of otherworldly players, going it in isolation. Trout's legacy will endure, as will those of Ohtani and even Pujols in this latter form, but the team they played for will be of little consequence or relevance. You may as well swap out the halos on the caps for the Pilots' long-neglected aerial motifs. In time, bereft of any memorable accomplishments or feats of their own, the Angels' significance to these stages of its stars' careers will be minimal. Trout, Ohtani, Pujols and now Rendon play in Anaheim. Outside of the Anaheim faithful (whose continued, obedient attendance suggests a Stockholm-lite Syndrome with their underperforming home team), who cares?

It would be easy to blame east coast bias for the neglect, or their also-ran status of late. They boast the game's brightest star, but Trout often rises to the occasion long after fans in earlier time zones have fallen asleep. Plus, those occasions of actual relevance are fewer and farther between than you'd like, given how little the Angels have mattered in the standings. Their efforts each year are undone by the type of unfortunate events fit for a children's series, but also by inadequacy; poor planning and poorer pitching. Causally the latter via the former. A never-ending slurry of disappointing, nondescript pitchers and middling supporting casts will earn you four consecutive sub-.500 seasons, certainly. But the question persists: Why do people keep showing up?

One answer is that, in some lights, the Angels are the most interesting team in baseball. Inadequacy might be at the forefront, but behind those failed efforts is, well, effort. That has been, in the last few seasons, a notable distinction from

Los Angeles Angels 2020

the rest of the league. Their 40-man payroll hasn't ended the season below $176 million since 2016. Their 26-man roster entering 2020 currently features four players earning more than $21 million (Trout, Pujols, Rendon, Upton), and a fifth (Simmons) at $15 million. They've amassed more singular talents than anyone else in the league: Trout is the best player in the game, possibly ever; Simmons is an ethereal defender and Ohtani is the premiere two-way player in baseball, whose prodigious talent on both sides of the ball demanded a rethinking of what is feasible within the modern game.

Framed a different way, it isn't as shocking as it might seem (based on their record) that a team who ranked in the top 10 in year-end payroll from 2004-13 has seen more than 3 million fans through their turnstiles every year since 2003. The Angels may be Lucy, but they can't be blamed for the fact that every fan is already, inherently, Charlie Brown. There's something virtuous in Charlie's hope, and so too in Lucy's determination to deny; even if Angels fans might have expected more coming into the season than another kick at the placed football, it still lingers, enticing the true believers.

The Angels, 3 million fans and all, are presently making no one care about a roster including Trout and Ohtani, Simmons and the remaining swings of Pujols. Even Rendon, with Trout's prime and his on the clock, might not be enough to quell the naysayers. Even so, they'll probably be entertained, even if they can't quite remember why. ■

—Ginny Searle is an author of Baseball Prospectus.

Part 2: Player Analysis

Los Angeles Angels 2020

PLAYER COMMENTS WITH GRAPHS

Justin Bour 1B
Born: 05/28/88 Age: 32 Bats: L Throws: R
Height: 6'4" Weight: 270 Origin: Round 25, 2009 Draft (#770 overall)

YEAR	TEAM	LVL	AGE	PA	R	2B	3B	HR	RBI	BB	K	SB	CS	AVG/OBP/SLG
2017	MIA	MLB	29	429	52	18	0	25	83	47	95	1	0	.289/.366/.536
2018	MIA	MLB	30	447	43	10	1	19	54	69	111	1	0	.227/.347/.412
2018	PHI	MLB	30	54	6	3	0	1	5	4	13	1	0	.224/.296/.347
2019	SLC	AAA	31	229	44	12	1	17	43	41	46	2	1	.316/.441/.663
2019	LAA	MLB	31	170	18	5	0	8	26	17	52	0	0	.172/.259/.364
2020	LAA	MLB	32	251	33	9	0	13	37	29	67	1	0	.238/.330/.464

Comparables: Brandon Belt, Justin Smoak, Steve Balboni

There's a scene in *Multiplicity*, 1996's sci-fi/fantasy comedy starring Michael Keaton (x4) where the original Keaton walks into a room to find that his two clones have created yet another clone. As the original panics, he also wonders, "What's up with #4?" #2 explains, "You know when you make a copy of a copy, it's not quite as sharp as the original?" Well, Bour was a copy of a copy of C.J. Cron's Angels tenure—a poorly applied patch among many for a lineup that never stopped leaking production from multiple holes. At a time when empty power has never been a more plentiful resource (pending the State of the Ball, of course), Bour has become part of MLB's latest wave of exports to Japan, signing with the Hanshin Tigers in November. Still no word on the contract status of the other clones, though.

YEAR	TEAM	LVL	AGE	PA	DRC+	VORP	BABIP	BRR	FRAA	WARP
2017	MIA	MLB	29	429	126	30.0	.322	-1.8	1B(102): -10.0	0.8
2018	MIA	MLB	30	447	103	14.8	.267	-3.1	1B(103): -6.3	-0.2
2018	PHI	MLB	30	54	103	-0.9	.286	0.2	1B(10): -0.5	0.1
2019	SLC	AAA	31	229	157	20.3	.339	-1.4	1B(25): -2.8	1.4
2019	LAA	MLB	31	170	77	-2.3	.196	-1.3		-0.4
2020	LAA	MLB	32	251	108	9.6	.279	-1.2	1B -4	0.6

Justin Bour, continued

Batted Ball Distribution

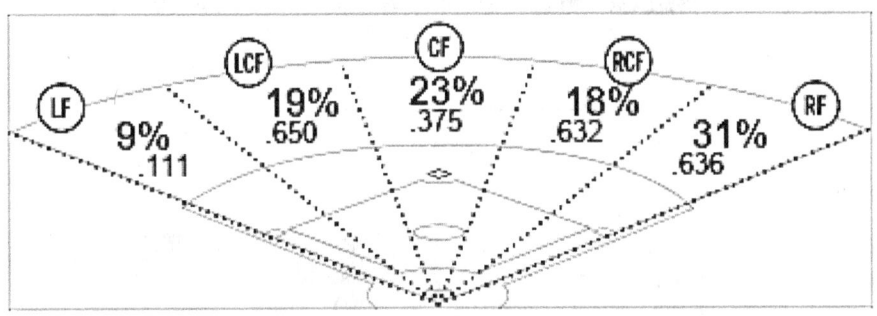

Strike Zone vs LHP **Strike Zone vs RHP**

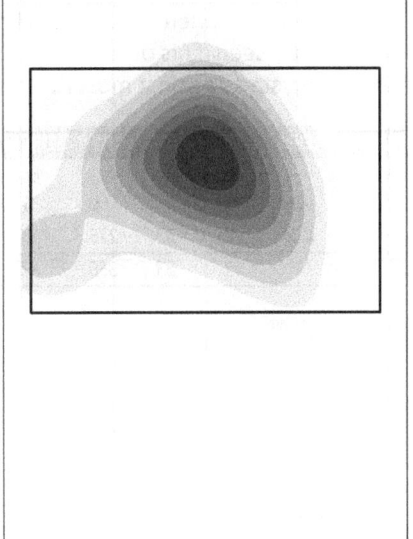

Jason Castro C

Born: 06/18/87 Age: 33 Bats: L Throws: R
Height: 6'3" Weight: 215 Origin: Round 1, 2008 Draft (#10 overall)

YEAR	TEAM	LVL	AGE	PA	R	2B	3B	HR	RBI	BB	K	SB	CS	AVG/OBP/SLG
2017	MIN	MLB	30	407	49	22	0	10	47	45	108	0	0	.242/.333/.388
2018	MIN	MLB	31	74	4	3	0	1	3	9	26	0	0	.143/.257/.238
2019	MIN	MLB	32	275	39	9	0	13	30	33	88	0	0	.232/.332/.435
2020	LAA	MLB	33	350	39	14	1	13	42	37	116	1	0	.214/.305/.389

Comparables: Rick Wilkins, Jorge Posada, Ron Karkovice

Castro bounced back in the last act of his three-year deal, posting his sixth twoish win season in his last seven. His script for success has turned: his defense has settled into very-good-not-quite-great middle age, while he posted the best DRC+ of his career thanks to a flyball-orientated shift in line with the rest of the Twins roster. It remains to be seen if his offensive gains will stick, but he should at least open 2020 getting starts against most right-handed pitchers.

YEAR	TEAM	P. COUNT	FRM RUNS	BLK RUNS	THRW RUNS	TOT RUNS
2017	MIN	14556	8.3	0.3	-0.2	8.1
2018	MIN	3132	1.4	0.9	0.1	2.2
2019	MIN	10672	6.1	-1.9	-0.3	3.8
2020	LAA	18622	8.3	-0.9	-0.9	6.5

YEAR	TEAM	LVL	AGE	PA	DRC+	VORP	BABIP	BRR	FRAA	WARP
2017	MIN	MLB	30	407	86	13.4	.318	-0.4	C(108): 7.7	2.1
2018	MIN	MLB	31	74	57	-2.3	.216	-0.7	C(19): 2.5	0.2
2019	MIN	MLB	32	275	100	14.7	.307	1.0	C(78): 3.5	1.9
2020	LAA	MLB	33	350	83	8.8	.295	0.0	C 6	1.5

Jason Castro, continued

Batted Ball Distribution

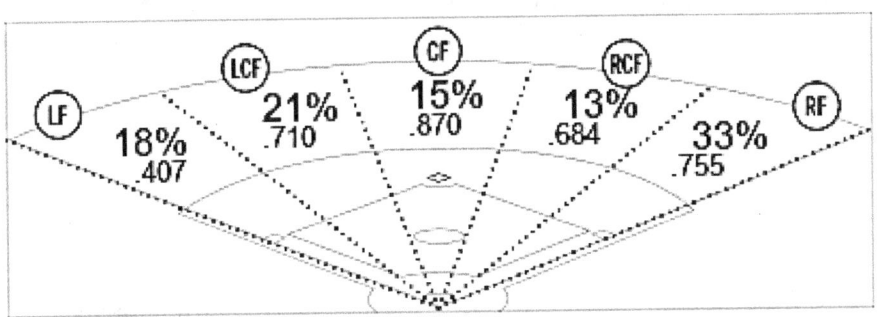

Strike Zone vs LHP **Strike Zone vs RHP**

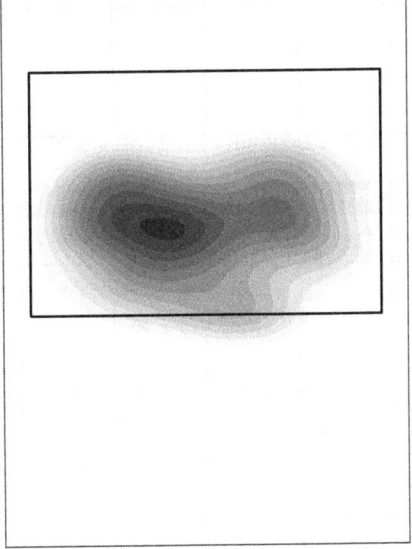

Los Angeles Angels 2020

David Fletcher UT
Born: 05/31/94 Age: 26 Bats: R Throws: R
Height: 5'9" Weight: 185 Origin: Round 6, 2015 Draft (#195 overall)

YEAR	TEAM	LVL	AGE	PA	R	2B	3B	HR	RBI	BB	K	SB	CS	AVG/OBP/SLG
2017	MOB	AA	23	272	32	14	1	1	22	21	30	12	5	.276/.341/.354
2017	SLC	AAA	23	217	27	6	1	2	17	6	25	8	1	.254/.285/.322
2018	SLC	AAA	24	275	55	25	5	6	37	16	21	7	2	.350/.394/.559
2018	LAA	MLB	24	307	35	18	2	1	25	15	34	3	0	.275/.316/.363
2019	LAA	MLB	25	653	83	30	4	6	49	55	64	8	3	.290/.350/.384
2020	LAA	MLB	26	525	50	27	2	7	50	36	61	10	3	.277/.331/.387

Comparables: Darwin Barney, Brent Butler, Aaron Hill

While The Beach Boys are a natural fit for Orange County's first professional sports team, Fletcher's jam isn't anything so obvious as "Surfin' USA" or "Wouldn't It Be Nice." No, you'll find the infielder sitting pensively by his locker, listening to *Pet Sounds* deep cut "I Just Wasn't Made for These Times." Fletcher, an OC native, would have been celebrated for his contact skills, excellent defense, and all-round grit in a bygone era. In the age of moonshots and megatools, he seems a quaint anachronism. But even if the skills are unfashionable, they propelled him to being the third-most valuable Angel in 2019. God only knows what the Angels will look like in 2020, but Fletcher's still bound to be giving his good vibrations.

YEAR	TEAM	LVL	AGE	PA	DRC+	VORP	BABIP	BRR	FRAA	WARP
2017	MOB	AA	23	272	115	9.6	.308	-1.5	2B(34): 1.0, SS(28): 0.0	1.3
2017	SLC	AAA	23	217	63	0.3	.281	2.3	SS(26): 0.2, 2B(22): 0.2	0.1
2018	SLC	AAA	24	275	135	24.4	.364	3.4	SS(31): 3.4, 2B(18): -1.6	3.0
2018	LAA	MLB	24	307	91	6.5	.307	3.5		1.6
2019	LAA	MLB	25	653	101	25.8	.317	-4.5		2.5
2020	LAA	MLB	26	525	91	13.1	.306	-0.5	2B 0, SS 0	1.6

David Fletcher, continued

Batted Ball Distribution

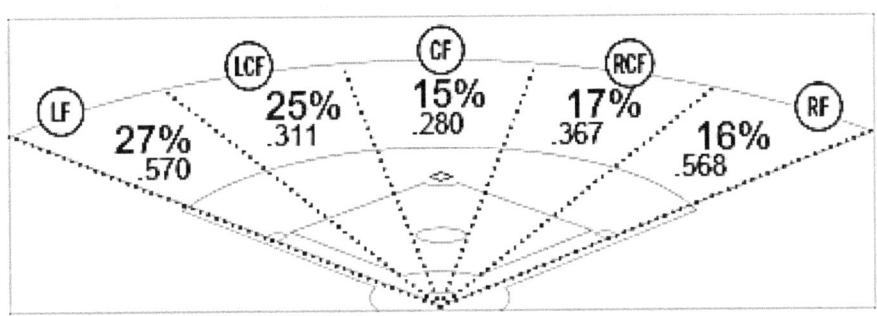

| Strike Zone vs LHP | Strike Zone vs RHP |

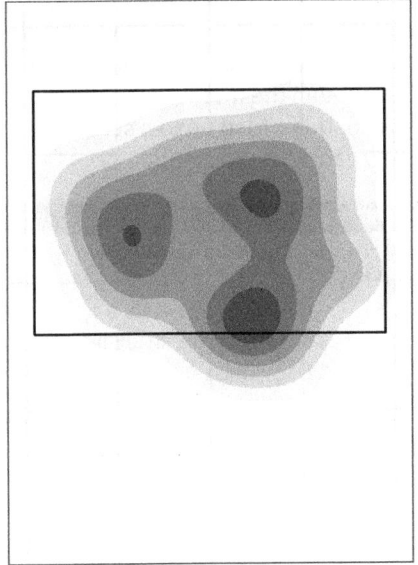
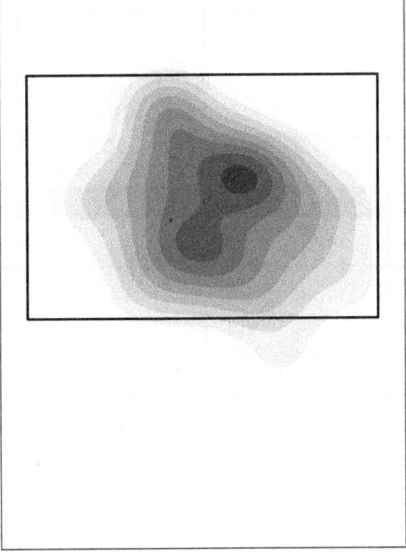

Angels Player Analysis - 23

Los Angeles Angels 2020

Brian Goodwin OF
Born: 11/02/90 Age: 29 Bats: L Throws: R
Height: 6'0" Weight: 200 Origin: Round 1, 2011 Draft (#34 overall)

YEAR	TEAM	LVL	AGE	PA	R	2B	3B	HR	RBI	BB	K	SB	CS	AVG/OBP/SLG
2017	SYR	AAA	26	103	9	4	0	2	11	10	29	2	1	.256/.327/.367
2017	WAS	MLB	26	278	41	21	1	13	30	23	69	6	0	.251/.313/.498
2018	OMA	AAA	27	44	6	4	0	2	9	4	11	0	0	.225/.295/.475
2018	WAS	MLB	27	79	9	1	0	3	12	10	26	3	1	.200/.321/.354
2018	KCA	MLB	27	101	11	5	0	3	13	6	31	1	1	.266/.317/.415
2019	LAA	MLB	28	458	65	29	3	17	47	38	129	7	3	.262/.326/.470
2020	LAA	MLB	29	525	60	24	2	21	68	45	156	10	3	.236/.306/.428

Comparables: Jake Marisnick, Craig Wilson, Robbie Grossman

With the prolonged absence of Justin Upton and the occasional absence of Mike Trout, spring training waiver claim Goodwin used 2019 to demonstrate that he was just good enough in full-time run to earn a more stable role as a fourth outfielder, able to competently hold down starting duties as needs dictate. Every aspect of his offensive game—power, plate discipline, speed—was similar to, if slightly better than, his prior part-time work over three seasons with the Nats and Royals. His defense wasn't terrible, though the metrics dinged his overuse as a jack-of-all-outfield-positions. All of this added up to a season in which, by WARP's lights, Goodwin very nearly earned his last name.

YEAR	TEAM	LVL	AGE	PA	DRC+	VORP	BABIP	BRR	FRAA	WARP
2017	SYR	AAA	26	103	91	0.3	.350	-1.6	RF(9): 0.8, CF(8): 0.0	0.0
2017	WAS	MLB	26	278	97	13.5	.291	0.1	CF(34): -1.2, LF(31): -0.2	0.8
2018	OMA	AAA	27	44	91	2.6	.259	0.1	CF(3): -0.5, RF(2): -0.4	0.1
2018	WAS	MLB	27	79	80	-0.6	.270	-1.8	LF(11): -0.2, RF(10): -0.7	-0.2
2018	KCA	MLB	27	101	84	3.5	.367	0.2	CF(25): -0.7, LF(1): -0.1	0.1
2019	LAA	MLB	28	458	100	13.7	.337	-1.3		0.9
2020	LAA	MLB	29	525	92	6.1	.304	-1.5	RF 6, CF -2	1.1

Brian Goodwin, continued

Batted Ball Distribution

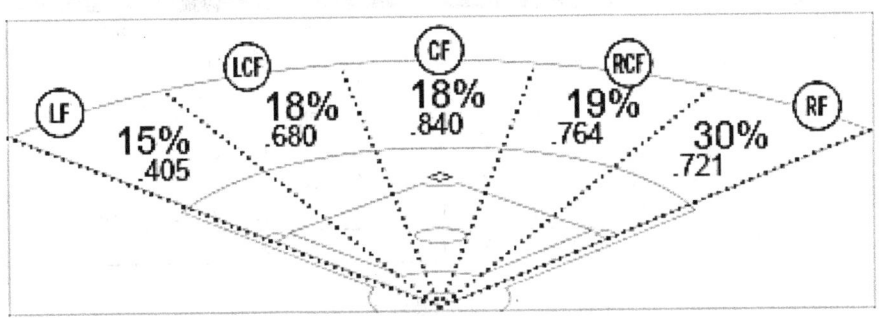

Strike Zone vs LHP   Strike Zone vs RHP

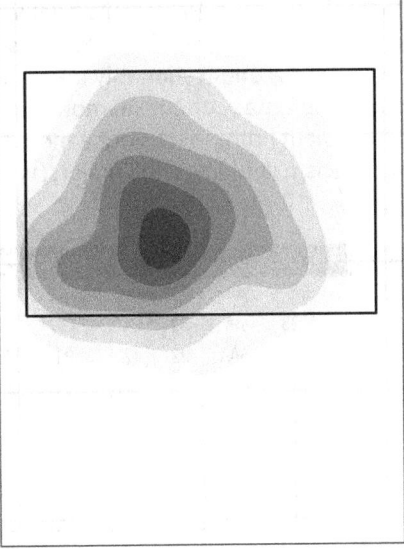

Los Angeles Angels 2020

Michael Hermosillo OF
Born: 01/17/95 Age: 25 Bats: R Throws: R
Height: 6'0" Weight: 205 Origin: Round 28, 2013 Draft (#847 overall)

YEAR	TEAM	LVL	AGE	PA	R	2B	3B	HR	RBI	BB	K	SB	CS	AVG/OBP/SLG
2017	INL	A+	22	64	5	6	0	0	2	9	15	5	2	.321/.438/.434
2017	MOB	AA	22	340	40	13	2	4	26	40	73	21	9	.248/.361/.353
2017	SLC	AAA	22	129	20	6	1	5	16	7	28	9	2	.287/.341/.487
2018	SLC	AAA	23	323	43	14	4	12	46	30	87	10	5	.267/.357/.480
2018	LAA	MLB	23	62	7	4	0	1	1	3	17	0	1	.211/.274/.333
2019	SLC	AAA	24	296	51	8	3	15	43	26	88	6	4	.243/.331/.471
2019	LAA	MLB	24	46	7	1	1	0	3	5	19	2	0	.139/.304/.222
2020	LAA	MLB	25	210	21	9	1	5	21	17	67	6	3	.214/.297/.351

Comparables: Mallex Smith, Brandon Nimmo, Billy McKinney

Biographically, Hermosillo is a one-man Proper Noun NAFTA, as the Ottawa, Illinois product shares a last name with a Mexican city and a hometown with the Canadian capital, all the while growing up in the Land of Lincoln. A high-school football standout, Hermosillo briefly occupied an Arizona Fall League dugout with fellow crossover Tim Tebow. It's not going too far on a limb to say that while Tebow unquestionably takes the gridiron honors, Hermosillo can easily claim supremacy on the diamond. You may think this is praise so faint as to be an ambient hum, so let's put a more positive spin on this: at least Hermosillo's athleticism got him to the majors, which is more than we can say for the other guy.

YEAR	TEAM	LVL	AGE	PA	DRC+	VORP	BABIP	BRR	FRAA	WARP
2017	INL	A+	22	64	161	4.3	.447	-1.3	CF(9): -2.3, LF(3): -0.3	0.2
2017	MOB	AA	22	340	119	14.5	.316	-2.0	CF(52): -2.3, RF(13): 2.3	1.5
2017	SLC	AAA	22	129	91	5.7	.337	0.3	LF(14): -0.1, CF(10): 0.6	0.4
2018	SLC	AAA	23	323	91	11.6	.341	-0.4	CF(36): 5.5, RF(19): 0.3	1.4
2018	LAA	MLB	23	62	61	-1.3	.282	-0.5		0.1
2019	SLC	AAA	24	296	72	11.1	.304	0.4	CF(40): 3.4, RF(11): -0.3	0.4
2019	LAA	MLB	24	46	62	-0.9	.278	0.8		0.0
2020	LAA	MLB	25	210	73	-1.4	.303	0.0	CF 0, LF 0	0.0

Michael Hermosillo, continued

Batted Ball Distribution

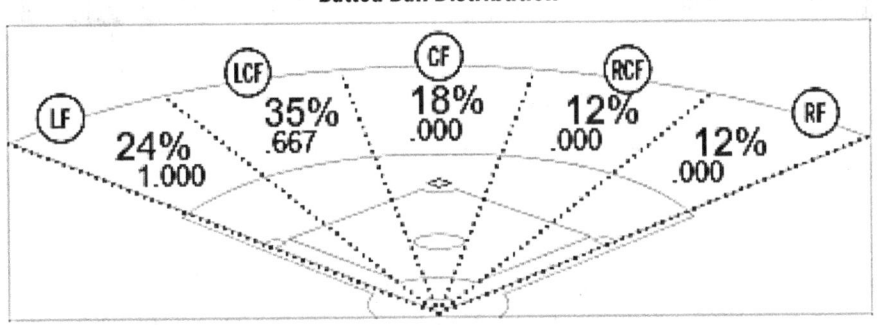

Strike Zone vs LHP   **Strike Zone vs RHP**

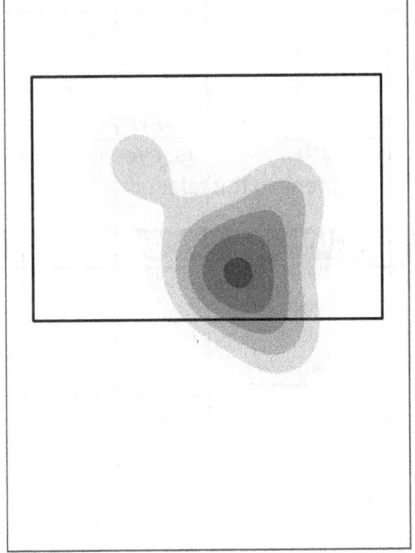

Los Angeles Angels 2020

Tommy La Stella   INF
Born: 01/31/89   Age: 31   Bats: L   Throws: R
Height: 5'11"   Weight: 180   Origin: Round 8, 2011 Draft (#266 overall)

YEAR	TEAM	LVL	AGE	PA	R	2B	3B	HR	RBI	BB	K	SB	CS	AVG/OBP/SLG
2017	IOW	AAA	28	121	14	2	0	1	6	10	22	0	1	.218/.281/.264
2017	CHN	MLB	28	151	18	8	0	5	22	20	18	0	0	.288/.389/.472
2018	CHN	MLB	29	192	23	8	0	1	19	17	27	0	1	.266/.340/.331
2019	LAA	MLB	30	321	49	8	0	16	44	20	28	0	0	.295/.346/.486
2020	LAA	MLB	31	385	43	17	1	12	46	33	46	2	1	.265/.335/.422

Comparables: Lou Whitaker, Luis Alicea, Phil Garner

Using *The Ball* as an explanation for an unexpected 2019 power breakout is fast becoming a tired, intellectually lazy argument. Forget the banality of everyday, materialist realism—we need myths to describe what happened to La Stella, who was an unassuming utility infielder with 10 career home runs and a .366 slugging percentage in over 900 major-league plate appearances coming into last season. He promptly went gonzo and jacked 16 bombs in a half-season until he launch-angled some extreme exit velocity off of his shin and succumbed to a broken tibia. Was the power a Faustian bargain? Icarus flying too close to the sun? While the Angels are filled to the brim with tantalizing storylines heading into 2020, one of the low-key more interesting ones will be the next installment of the myth of La Stella, even if *The Ball* ends up being the all-too-prosaic denouement to the tale.

YEAR	TEAM	LVL	AGE	PA	DRC+	VORP	BABIP	BRR	FRAA	WARP
2017	IOW	AAA	28	121	56	-3.5	.261	1.0	2B(22): 0.3, 3B(4): 0.0	-0.1
2017	CHN	MLB	28	151	114	11.6	.298	-0.7	2B(21): -2.4, 3B(18): -0.5	0.4
2018	CHN	MLB	29	192	84	3.1	.312	0.7	3B(26): -1.8, 2B(15): 0.3	0.2
2019	LAA	MLB	30	321	119	19.2	.282	-1.0		1.5
2020	LAA	MLB	31	385	101	10.7	.277	-0.3	1B -1, 2B -2	0.7

Tommy La Stella, continued

Batted Ball Distribution

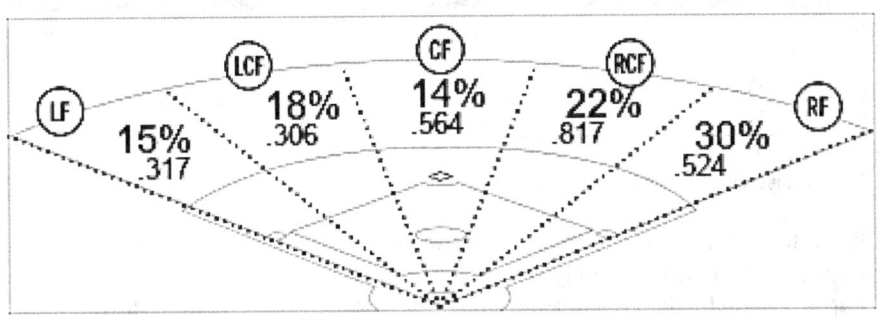

Strike Zone vs LHP   **Strike Zone vs RHP**

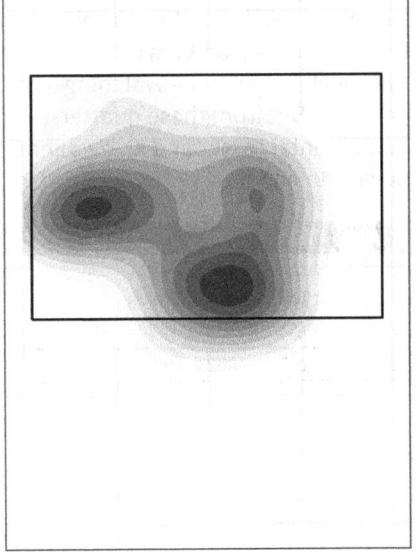

Albert Pujols 1B

Born: 01/16/80 Age: 40 Bats: R Throws: R
Height: 6'3" Weight: 235 Origin: Round 13, 1999 Draft (#402 overall)

YEAR	TEAM	LVL	AGE	PA	R	2B	3B	HR	RBI	BB	K	SB	CS	AVG/OBP/SLG
2017	LAA	MLB	37	636	53	17	0	23	101	37	93	3	0	.241/.286/.386
2018	LAA	MLB	38	498	50	20	0	19	64	28	65	1	0	.245/.289/.411
2019	LAA	MLB	39	545	55	22	0	23	93	43	68	3	0	.244/.305/.430
2020	LAA	MLB	40	490	55	21	0	20	64	34	70	3	1	.241/.299/.423

Comparables: Chipper Jones, Scott Rolen, Eric Chavez

It would be easy to add another pile of snark onto the mountain of derision that Pujols' contract with the Angels has garnered since months after ink was put to paper back in the first Obama administration. What Pujols' 2019 performance makes clear, however, is that the 40-year-old has no desire to hobble gently into that good night. 2019 both held an uptick in plate appearances and was the second year running that, by DRC+, he's bobbed within the standard deviation of a league-average bat. And while largely irrelevant to his team's (lack of) success, the fact that the oft-injured DH stole three bases at least suggests a fierce wish to inhabit his younger body, if only for a short moment likely to lead to a much longer pain. Watching a generational talent decline is no fun for anybody. But from these quarters, Pujols gets nothing but respect: both for a monumental career and an evident desire to do everything within his dwindling powers to end it as a productive player.

YEAR	TEAM	LVL	AGE	PA	DRC+	VORP	BABIP	BRR	FRAA	WARP
2017	LAA	MLB	37	636	90	-17.5	.249	-1.2	1B(6): -0.6	-0.1
2018	LAA	MLB	38	498	101	0.9	.247	-1.9		1.0
2019	LAA	MLB	39	545	98	7.2	.238	-5.0		0.2
2020	LAA	MLB	40	490	87	-2.5	.245	-2.2	1B 0	-0.3

Albert Pujols, continued

Batted Ball Distribution

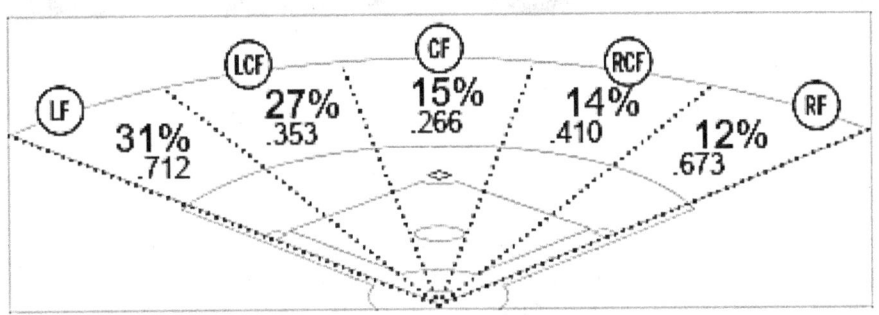

Strike Zone vs LHP

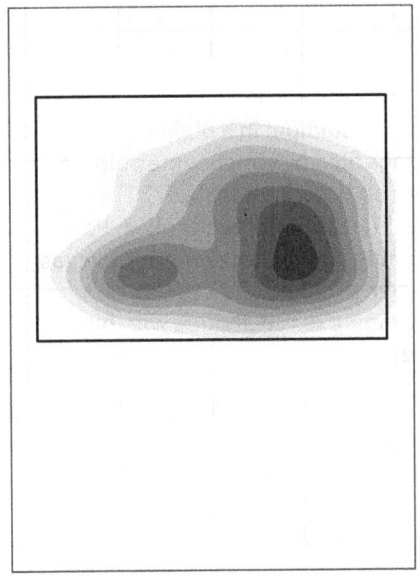

Strike Zone vs RHP

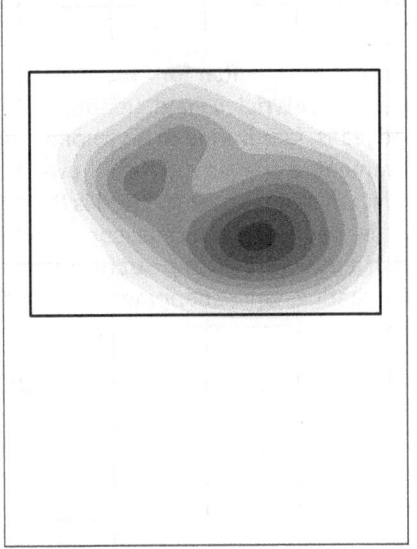

Anthony Rendon 3B

Born: 06/06/90 Age: 30 Bats: R Throws: R
Height: 6'1" Weight: 200 Origin: Round 1, 2011 Draft (#6 overall)

YEAR	TEAM	LVL	AGE	PA	R	2B	3B	HR	RBI	BB	K	SB	CS	AVG/OBP/SLG
2017	WAS	MLB	27	605	81	41	1	25	100	84	82	7	2	.301/.403/.533
2018	WAS	MLB	28	597	88	44	2	24	92	55	82	2	1	.308/.374/.535
2019	WAS	MLB	29	646	117	44	3	34	126	80	86	5	1	.319/.412/.598
2020	LAA	MLB	30	630	82	37	1	26	88	72	99	7	3	.279/.371/.493

Comparables: Steve Buechele, David Wright, Edwin Encarnación

The most "Rendon" moment of the season didn't come when he deposited a Zack Greinke center-cut changeup into the Crawford Boxes during Game 7 of the World Series. Or when he took Clayton Kershaw deep in Game 5 of the NLDS. Or any of the 44 league-leading doubles he slapped, as easy as you please, all over the field. Or any of the runs he drove in; in any of the walks that in aggregate nearly eclipsed his strikeout total. In any of the pitches he took in the shadow of the zone or incredible, league-leading side-eyes at called strikes that were well off the plate. If Rendon didn't swing at it, it probably wasn't a strike.

No, the most "Rendon" moment of the season came in an August sweep of the Cubs at Wrigley Field, Rendon entering the stadium in a plain white T-shirt and jeans, face buried in his phone. Cubs fans filed by him; no one pointed or commented or even did the elbow-whisper of, "Hey, isn't that ... ?" There's a point where being underrated is the same thing as being overlooked. Rendon will be neither after last season, an MVP candidate who lacks Harper's Vegas flash and showmanship but nevertheless commands attention, that fast, devastating, wrist-snapping swing of his seeming to run at odds with his easygoing, occasionally sardonic presence.

Perhaps the only room for improvement in his game is fielding, though zoned and unzoned rating systems appear to disagree about its quality. Rendon himself has joked that fielding behind Washington's strikeout-emphasizing pitching staff was "boring." He'll certainly face more challenges (and balls in play) in Anaheim over the next eight years, but one thing is guaranteed: watching him will be anything but.

YEAR	TEAM	LVL	AGE	PA	DRC+	VORP	BABIP	BRR	FRAA	WARP
2017	WAS	MLB	27	605	139	63.4	.314	2.0	3B(145): -1.6	5.2
2018	WAS	MLB	28	597	134	60.1	.323	2.9	3B(136): -5.7	4.4
2019	WAS	MLB	29	646	150	67.8	.323	1.0	3B(146): -4.5, 2B(1): 0.0	6.3
2020	LAA	MLB	30	630	125	36.9	.299	1.4	3B -3	3.5

Anthony Rendon, continued

Batted Ball Distribution

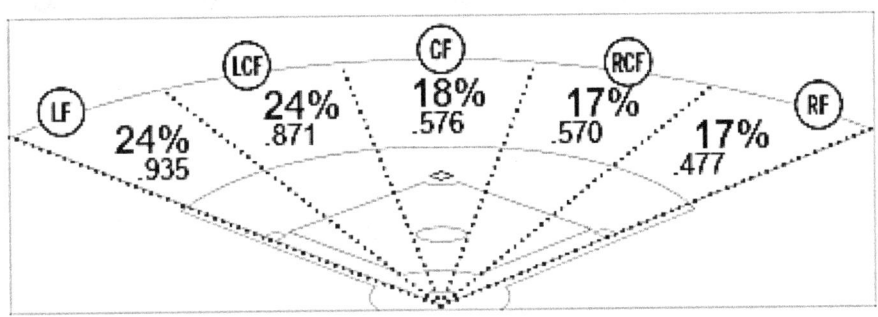

Strike Zone vs LHP   **Strike Zone vs RHP**

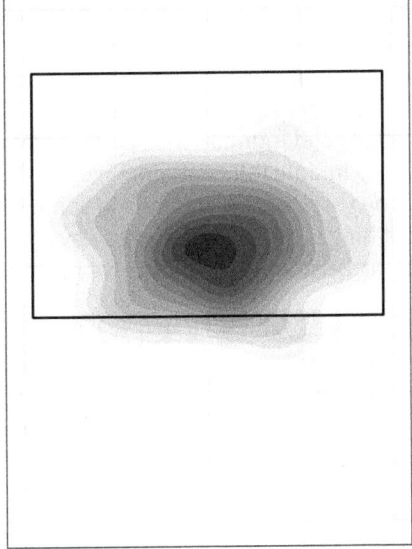

Los Angeles Angels 2020

Luis Rengifo 2B
Born: 02/26/97 Age: 23 Bats: B Throws: R
Height: 5'10" Weight: 195 Origin: International Free Agent, 2013

YEAR	TEAM	LVL	AGE	PA	R	2B	3B	HR	RBI	BB	K	SB	CS	AVG/OBP/SLG
2017	CLN	A	20	450	65	24	4	11	44	33	80	29	14	.250/.318/.413
2017	BGR	A	20	104	14	3	1	1	8	8	17	5	3	.250/.308/.333
2018	INL	A+	21	190	36	11	3	2	16	27	22	22	8	.323/.426/.466
2018	MOB	AA	21	181	37	10	5	2	21	23	22	13	2	.305/.420/.477
2018	SLC	AAA	21	219	36	9	5	3	27	25	31	6	6	.274/.358/.421
2019	SLC	AAA	22	122	16	4	1	5	14	11	24	3	3	.273/.336/.464
2019	LAA	MLB	22	406	44	18	3	7	33	40	93	2	5	.238/.321/.364
2020	LAA	MLB	23	210	21	8	1	5	21	18	48	8	4	.228/.301/.360

Comparables: Dalton Pompey, Luis Urías, Jesmuel Valentín

If you're not a close follower of the Angels, you may not remember that, among the seemingly endless list of misfortunes suffered by the club in 2019, Rengifo was lost in the middle of September to a broken hamate bone in his left hand. Hamates can be a notoriously tricky rehab, and some players (looking at you, Pablo Sandoval) never fully get their mojo back. Assuming Rengifo can be ready to roll by spring, however, he'll be looking to build on a promising rookie season. The stat line doesn't wow, but he does a lot of things well, and it comes with a solid foundation: a patient plate approach and impressive athletic ability in the middle infield. Before we cast him into the "utility" bin, there's reason to hope for growth in power and some more game speed on the bases as well. The bat hinges on the hamate, however, so here's hoping Rengifo can benefit from some karmic redistribution for baseball's unluckiest 2019 club.

YEAR	TEAM	LVL	AGE	PA	DRC+	VORP	BABIP	BRR	FRAA	WARP
2017	CLN	A	20	450	107	22.0	.285	4.3	SS(31): -2.8, 2B(25): 2.8	2.4
2017	BGR	A	20	104	110	6.0	.295	0.4	SS(23): -1.5	0.9
2018	INL	A+	21	190	173	28.1	.365	2.5	SS(36): 3.9, 2B(2): 0.0	2.8
2018	MOB	AA	21	181	146	14.2	.346	-1.0	SS(30): -3.4, 2B(9): -0.8	1.1
2018	SLC	AAA	21	219	112	12.0	.310	3.3	2B(31): -1.5, SS(16): 0.1	1.3
2019	SLC	AAA	22	122	77	2.7	.305	-0.4	SS(12): 0.9, 2B(12): 3.6	0.5
2019	LAA	MLB	22	406	84	5.8	.300	-0.4		0.5
2020	LAA	MLB	23	210	78	2.2	.282	-0.1	2B 0, SS 0	0.2

Luis Rengifo, continued

Batted Ball Distribution

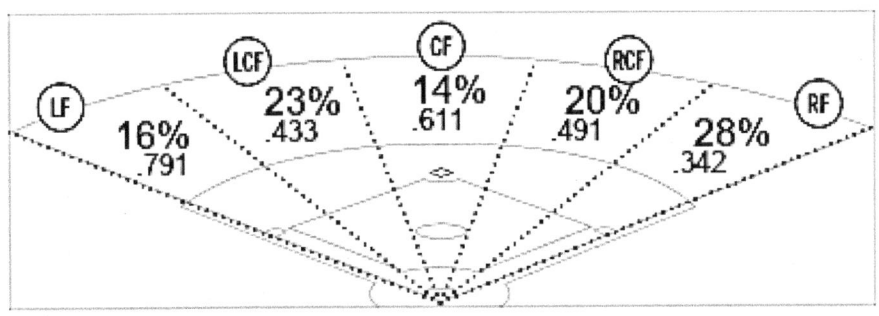

Strike Zone vs LHP   **Strike Zone vs RHP**

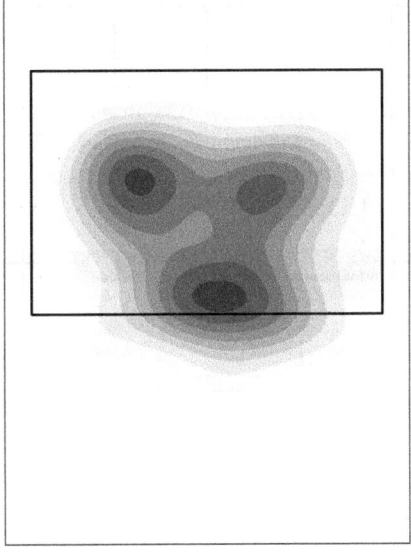

Andrelton Simmons SS

Born: 09/04/89   Age: 30   Bats: R   Throws: R
Height: 6'2"   Weight: 195   Origin: Round 2, 2010 Draft (#70 overall)

YEAR	TEAM	LVL	AGE	PA	R	2B	3B	HR	RBI	BB	K	SB	CS	AVG/OBP/SLG
2017	LAA	MLB	27	647	77	38	2	14	69	47	67	19	6	.278/.331/.421
2018	LAA	MLB	28	600	68	26	5	11	75	35	44	10	2	.292/.337/.417
2019	LAA	MLB	29	424	47	19	0	7	40	24	37	10	2	.264/.309/.364
2020	LAA	MLB	30	595	56	28	2	10	58	37	59	10	3	.263/.313/.374

Comparables: Barry Larkin, Bill Russell, José Reyes

The perennial Gold Glover and Resident Fielding Wizard, Simmons once again returned to elite leather levels if you look at the metrics alone. But defensive stats are a tricky business, and even at their best they give only a partial, blinkered view. First of all, Simmons' 2018 down year, FRAA-ly speaking, was mainly due to a reduction of overall chances, not any downturn in fielding acumen. And 2019 was spoiled almost from the get-go by a nagging ankle sprain and related injuries to tendons and bone. Offensively, this made it hard for Simmons to take advantage of the funtime happyball, and he stepped back from the hitting gains of the previous two seasons. But let's not forget the fortitude of a player who, bum ankle and all, managed a fielding season that graded out (in only 103 games!) as the second-best among shortstops—oh, while stealing 10 bags, too. Health, and with it a rebound to league-average offense, should return Simmons to his rightful place as one of the most valuable shortstops in the league.

YEAR	TEAM	LVL	AGE	PA	DRC+	VORP	BABIP	BRR	FRAA	WARP
2017	LAA	MLB	27	647	102	32.3	.291	2.7	SS(158): 16.1	5.0
2018	LAA	MLB	28	600	107	35.1	.300	3.8		2.9
2019	LAA	MLB	29	424	81	9.9	.277	-0.1		2.0
2020	LAA	MLB	30	595	82	10.0	.279	1.4	SS 6	1.6

Andrelton Simmons, continued

Batted Ball Distribution

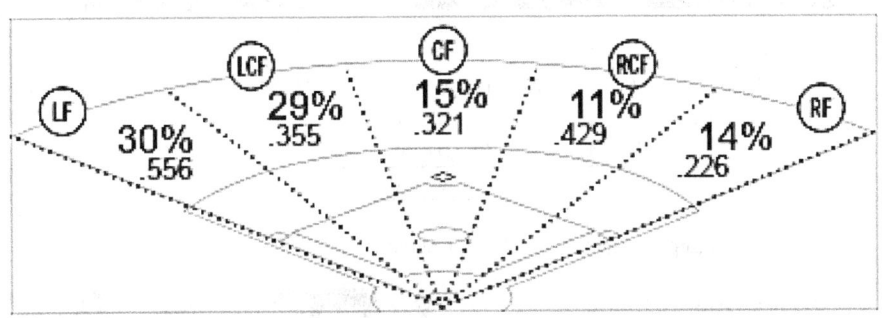

Strike Zone vs LHP   **Strike Zone vs RHP**

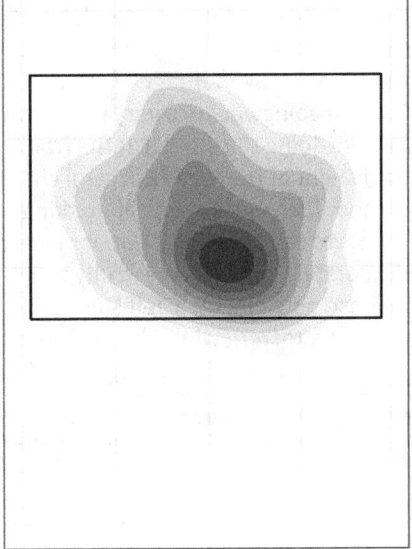

Los Angeles Angels 2020

Max Stassi C
Born: 03/15/91 Age: 29 Bats: R Throws: R
Height: 5'10" Weight: 200 Origin: Round 4, 2009 Draft (#123 overall)

YEAR	TEAM	LVL	AGE	PA	R	2B	3B	HR	RBI	BB	K	SB	CS	AVG/OBP/SLG
2017	FRE	AAA	26	287	54	14	0	12	33	38	67	1	1	.266/.383/.473
2017	HOU	MLB	26	31	5	1	0	2	4	6	4	0	0	.167/.323/.458
2018	HOU	MLB	27	250	28	13	0	8	27	23	74	0	0	.226/.316/.394
2019	HOU	MLB	28	98	4	1	0	1	3	7	34	0	0	.167/.235/.211
2019	LAA	MLB	28	49	3	0	0	0	2	5	15	0	0	.071/.163/.071
2020	LAA	MLB	29	280	28	12	0	10	32	22	91	0	0	.207/.281/.370

Comparables: Mike Carp, Jake Marisnick, John Ryan Murphy

For those of you hip to the Gen-Z catcher-framing metrics here at BP, you've probably had Stassi on your short list of crushes for a while: Last season, his framing saved more runs than J.T. Realmuto—in fewer than one-third as many chances. Somewhere, there's a TikTok montage of Stassi's framing going viral in a very niche way

YEAR	TEAM	P. COUNT	FRM RUNS	BLK RUNS	THRW RUNS	TOT RUNS
2017	FRE	9878	11.4	0.0	-0.8	10.1
2017	HOU	1029	0.2	0.4	0.0	0.5
2018	HOU	9540	13.9	0.1	-0.1	14.0
2019	HOU	3717	6.6	-0.2	-0.1	6.3
2019	LAA	2392	3.9	-0.5	-0.1	3.3
2020	LAA	11239	4.7	0.3	-0.3	4.7

(are we doing this right?). If the framing is *au courant*, however, the bat is the equivalent of the Steve Buscemi character from *30 Rock*, skateboard slung over his shoulder, enthusiastically asking his "fellow" high school kids how they do. That is to say, awkward, out of place, and redolent of a 40-something desperately and unsuccessfully trying to keep up with the youngsters. The defense puts him on a Jeff Mathis-like career trajectory (forever young, or at least on a roster), while the bat looks to age as well as that MySpace background you thought was kind of edgy in 2005.

YEAR	TEAM	LVL	AGE	PA	DRC+	VORP	BABIP	BRR	FRAA	WARP
2017	FRE	AAA	26	287	125	27.0	.321	-0.2	C(65): 10.8	3.2
2017	HOU	MLB	26	31	106	0.9	.105	0.0	C(11): 0.5, 1B(1): 0.0	0.2
2018	HOU	MLB	27	250	86	9.6	.302	-0.1	C(82): 14.5	2.3
2019	HOU	MLB	28	98	61	0.1	.255	-1.3	C(26): 6.1, 1B(3): 0.0	0.5
2019	LAA	MLB	28	49	24	-2.3	.103	0.0		0.1
2020	LAA	MLB	29	280	72	2.3	.281	-0.5	C 5	0.7

Max Stassi, continued

Batted Ball Distribution

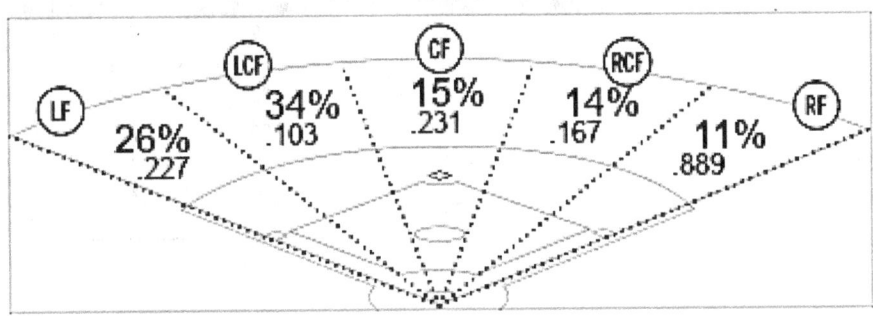

Strike Zone vs LHP

Strike Zone vs RHP

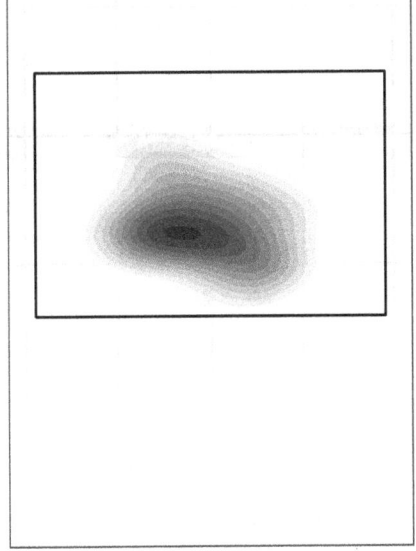

Matt Thaiss CI

Born: 05/06/95   Age: 25   Bats: L   Throws: R
Height: 6'0"   Weight: 215   Origin: Round 1, 2016 Draft (#16 overall)

YEAR	TEAM	LVL	AGE	PA	R	2B	3B	HR	RBI	BB	K	SB	CS	AVG/OBP/SLG
2017	INL	A+	22	385	46	13	4	8	48	40	59	4	3	.265/.353/.399
2017	MOB	AA	22	221	29	14	0	1	25	37	50	4	3	.292/.412/.388
2018	MOB	AA	23	176	24	10	2	6	25	16	35	2	1	.287/.352/.490
2018	SLC	AAA	23	400	54	24	6	10	51	28	68	6	3	.277/.328/.457
2019	SLC	AAA	24	372	63	17	2	14	49	59	64	1	0	.274/.390/.477
2019	LAA	MLB	24	164	17	7	0	8	23	17	52	0	0	.211/.293/.422
2020	LAA	MLB	25	105	12	4	0	4	13	11	27	1	0	.230/.314/.401

Comparables: Yonder Alonso, Max Muncy, Brett Wallace

Every once in a while a first base prospect without hammerhead power swims against the current of probability and makes it to the far shore of the majors. Thaiss reached that beachhead in 2019, though he floundered a bit once he came ashore. It remains to be seen if the hit tool will play enough to give him some oxygen, and if the power is enough to reach dry land. If his 2019 is any indication, we already know his approach has evolved enough for him walk just fine.

YEAR	TEAM	LVL	AGE	PA	DRC+	VORP	BABIP	BRR	FRAA	WARP
2017	INL	A+	22	385	120	13.7	.299	0.5	1B(78): 2.8	1.6
2017	MOB	AA	22	221	158	11.5	.389	-1.2	1B(46): -1.5	1.2
2018	MOB	AA	23	176	125	9.0	.331	-1.1	1B(36): 2.6	0.8
2018	SLC	AAA	23	400	95	-0.6	.314	0.2	1B(77): 5.4	0.9
2019	SLC	AAA	24	372	109	18.8	.303	1.3	3B(47): -2.5, 1B(23): -1.4	1.2
2019	LAA	MLB	24	164	91	3.7	.264	-1.6		-0.1
2020	LAA	MLB	25	105	90	0.4	.283	-0.2	1B 1	0.1

Matt Thaiss, continued

Batted Ball Distribution

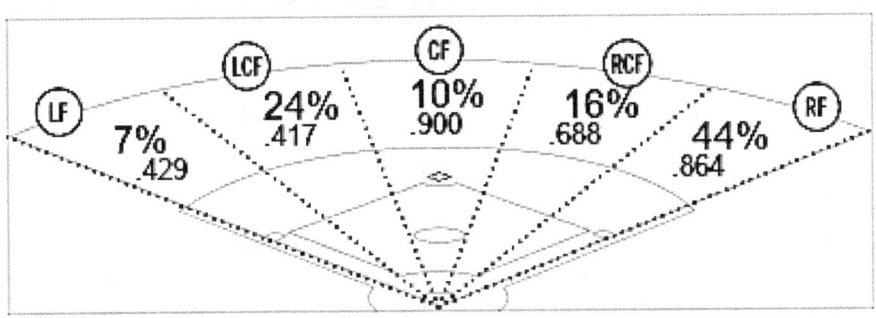

Strike Zone vs LHP   Strike Zone vs RHP

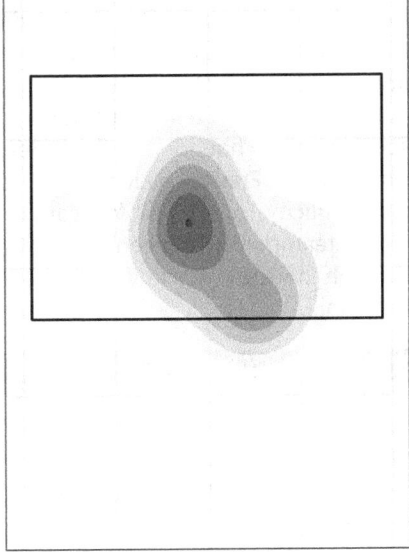

Los Angeles Angels 2020

Mike Trout CF
Born: 08/07/91   Age: 28   Bats: R   Throws: R
Height: 6'2"   Weight: 235   Origin: Round 1, 2009 Draft (#25 overall)

YEAR	TEAM	LVL	AGE	PA	R	2B	3B	HR	RBI	BB	K	SB	CS	AVG/OBP/SLG
2017	LAA	MLB	25	507	92	25	3	33	72	94	90	22	4	.306/.442/.629
2018	LAA	MLB	26	608	101	24	4	39	79	122	124	24	2	.312/.460/.628
2019	LAA	MLB	27	600	110	27	2	45	104	110	120	11	2	.291/.438/.645
2020	LAA	MLB	28	630	114	27	3	48	124	110	138	19	6	.298/.435/.645

Comparables: Giancarlo Stanton, Bryce Harper, Rick Monday

It's hard to be mad at Mike Trout for being the most unassuming "greatest player of his generation" in baseball's (or really, any sport's) history. His performance continues to outclass virtually all of his peers, and any statistical variations (say, the reduction of steals) seem less like a cause for concern than an effortless toggling between different genres of perfection, a DJ of baseball godhead on the ones and twos. He even turned a potential free-agency circus into an acoustic set on a side stage, inking a 12-year, $430 million contract extension with little fanfare on a Wednesday in March, presumably making him a lifelong Angel. Trout also resists being a headliner among the league's impressive lineup of young stars: in its "Let the Kids Play" ad, an attempt to market its faces for a new generation, Trout recedes to the background, only speaking when hounded by "reporters," letting the gregarious swagger of Alex Bregman and Francisco Lindor take center stage. One could surmise that the only publicity Trout might feel comfortable with is hoisting a trophy with his Angels teammates. The generationally-talented centerpiece is firmly in place through the 2020s; it's now up to Moreno, Eppler and Co. to find the perfect ensemble.

YEAR	TEAM	LVL	AGE	PA	DRC+	VORP	BABIP	BRR	FRAA	WARP
2017	LAA	MLB	25	507	176	69.9	.318	0.0	CF(108): -3.3	6.2
2018	LAA	MLB	26	608	183	91.0	.346	1.5		8.2
2019	LAA	MLB	27	600	177	81.5	.298	3.4		8.9
2020	LAA	MLB	28	630	177	85.6	.322	0.2	CF -3	8.6

Mike Trout, continued

Batted Ball Distribution

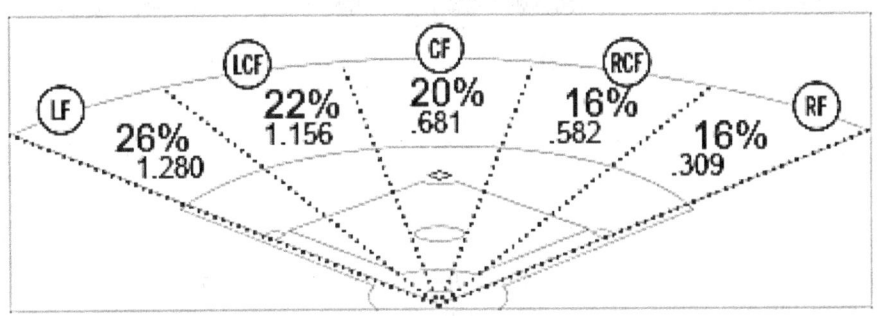

Strike Zone vs LHP   **Strike Zone vs RHP**

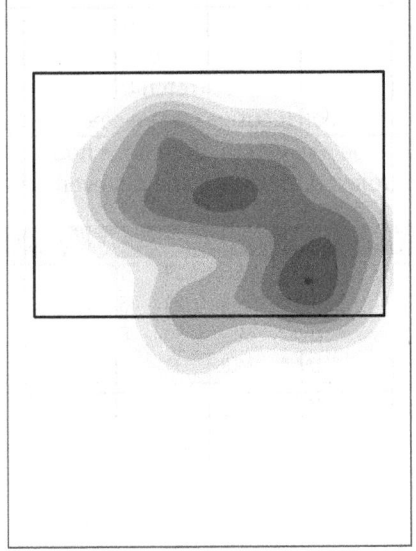

Los Angeles Angels 2020

Justin Upton LF

Born: 08/25/87 Age: 32 Bats: R Throws: R
Height: 6'1" Weight: 215 Origin: Round 1, 2005 Draft (#1 overall)

YEAR	TEAM	LVL	AGE	PA	R	2B	3B	HR	RBI	BB	K	SB	CS	AVG/OBP/SLG
2017	LAA	MLB	29	115	19	7	0	7	15	17	33	4	0	.245/.357/.531
2017	DET	MLB	29	520	81	37	0	28	94	57	147	10	5	.279/.362/.542
2018	LAA	MLB	30	613	80	18	1	30	85	64	176	8	2	.257/.344/.463
2019	LAA	MLB	31	256	34	8	0	12	40	32	78	1	1	.215/.309/.416
2020	LAA	MLB	32	560	76	24	1	31	86	62	173	10	4	.245/.334/.486

Comparables: Andruw Jones, Mike Cameron, Jay Bruce

At some point, almost imperceptibly, Upton went from being a young, promising player to a grizzled veteran. It probably happened somewhere in his odyssey to four different clubs in five years, between the 2013 viral image, riffing off of DMX, proclaiming a fraternal Atlanta outfield of "Upton here! Upton here!" and landing his last big payday to patrol left field and swat bombs in Anaheim through his age-34 season. Lest we write career eulogies too soon, Upton's 2019 was a total write-off, as he battled toe and knee woes from the spring right through September. Upton is still young and talented enough to come back and enjoy a productive stretch through his mid-30s, and a now-broken track record of eight consecutive 600 PA seasons backs this up. He is also old enough that we'd be naïve to think that his hobbled 2019 doesn't remind us that even the sturdiest bodies can, and do, eventually break down.

YEAR	TEAM	LVL	AGE	PA	DRC+	VORP	BABIP	BRR	FRAA	WARP
2017	LAA	MLB	29	115	131	7.7	.293	1.1	LF(27): -2.6	0.6
2017	DET	MLB	29	520	129	32.1	.351	-0.6	LF(124): 11.8	4.3
2018	LAA	MLB	30	613	117	32.6	.321	-1.6		4.4
2019	LAA	MLB	31	256	91	3.8	.261	0.5		0.1
2020	LAA	MLB	32	560	113	23.3	.310	-0.4	LF 10	3.5

Justin Upton, continued

Batted Ball Distribution

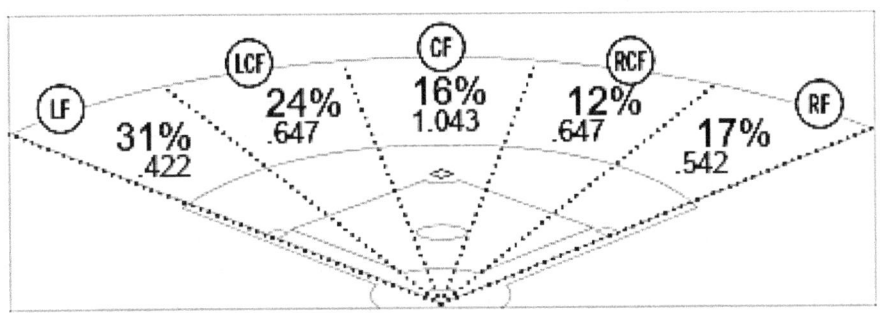

Strike Zone vs LHP   **Strike Zone vs RHP**

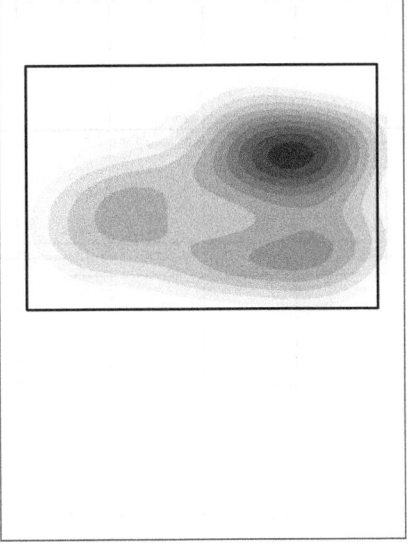

Los Angeles Angels 2020

Justin Anderson RHP
Born: 09/28/92   Age: 27   Bats: L   Throws: R
Height: 6'3"   Weight: 230   Origin: Round 14, 2014 Draft (#419 overall)

YEAR	TEAM	LVL	AGE	W	L	SV	G	GS	IP	H	HR	BB/9	K/9	K	GB%	BABIP
2017	MOB	AA	24	3	2	1	42	0	58^2	56	7	4.4	5.5	36	49%	.266
2018	LAA	MLB	25	3	3	4	57	0	55^1	42	3	6.5	10.9	67	54%	.310
2019	LAA	MLB	26	3	0	1	54	0	47	42	6	6.1	11.5	60	36%	.305
2020	LAA	MLB	27	2	2	0	40	0	43	36	6	5.0	11.3	54	42%	.297

Comparables: Jake Jewell, Colten Brewer, Phillips Valdez

The hard-throwing righty began 2019 with five scoreless appearances in the season's first 10 days and was promptly rewarded with ... the closer's job, you say? Well, no, the Angels had to wait until the final frames of the Cody Allen disaster film before making the switch to Hansel Robles. No, Anderson's sterling start was rewarded with a head-scratching demotion to Triple-A Salt Lake City. Upon his return from a short stint at the foot of the Wasatch, the early-April magic dissipated in a fog of inconsistency, with poor command being the main culprit. Heading into his age-27 season, Anderson's time to become a late-inning fireballer, rather than cannon fodder, is rapidly approaching the zero hour.

YEAR	TEAM	LVL	AGE	WHIP	ERA	DRA	WARP	MPH	FB%	WHF	CSP
2017	MOB	AA	24	1.45	5.06	6.04	-0.9				
2018	LAA	MLB	25	1.48	4.07	4.52	0.3	99.5	44.7	14.4	42.2
2019	LAA	MLB	26	1.57	5.55	4.86	0.3	96.3	47.1	12.8	42.4
2020	LAA	MLB	27	1.40	4.33	4.36	0.4	97.4	46.5	13.7	42.8

Justin Anderson, continued

Pitch Shape vs LHH

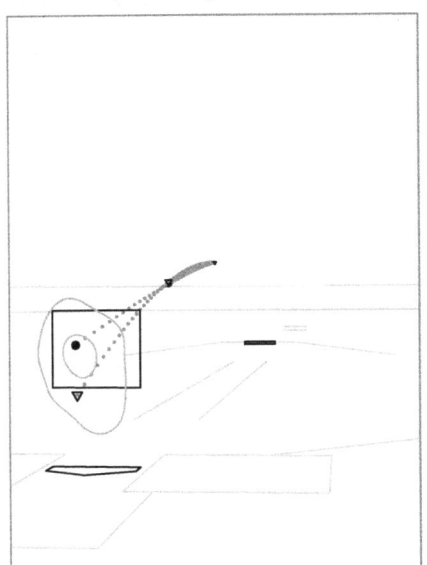

Pitch Shape vs RHH

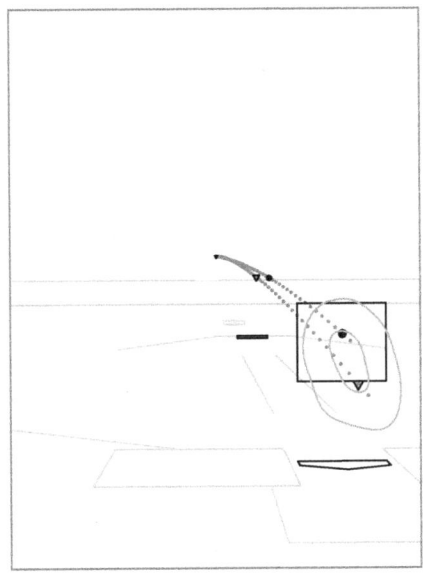

Type	Frequency	Velocity	H Movement	V Movement
● Fastball	45.5%	95.1 [108]	-6.5 [101]	-12.7 [108]
☐ Sinker				
+ Cutter				
▲ Changeup				
✗ Splitter				
▽ Slider	51.7%	84.9 [102]	7.8 [111]	-31.2 [106]
◇ Curveball				
⊕ Slow Curveball				
✱ Knuckleball				
▼ Screwball				

Matt Andriese RHP

Born: 08/28/89   Age: 30   Bats: R   Throws: R
Height: 6'2"   Weight: 225   Origin: Round 3, 2011 Draft (#112 overall)

YEAR	TEAM	LVL	AGE	W	L	SV	G	GS	IP	H	HR	BB/9	K/9	K	GB%	BABIP
2017	TBA	MLB	27	5	5	1	18	17	86	90	16	2.9	8.0	76	46%	.296
2018	TBA	MLB	28	3	4	0	27	4	59^2	55	7	2.7	8.9	59	52%	.291
2018	ARI	MLB	28	0	3	0	14	1	19	29	8	3.3	9.0	19	44%	.382
2019	ARI	MLB	29	5	5	1	54	0	70^2	72	8	3.4	10.1	79	51%	.333
2020	ARI	MLB	30	3	3	0	58	0	61	57	9	2.7	8.9	61	48%	.292

Comparables: Chase Whitley, Cody Martin, Jake Buchanan

Sometimes, less is more. That's what both the Diamondbacks and Andriese learned during a 2019 season that can confidently be described as the best of his career. The right-hander seemed, for most of his career, to be nothing more than your prototypical swing-man. Last season he settled in as a reliable middle reliever who misses enough bats to survive in today's game and generates enough ground balls to thrive. He did so by simplifying his repertoire, ditching his cutter almost entirely for a fastball-changeup combo that has always been tough for hitters to differentiate between. Control issues still limit his ceiling, but Andriese seems to have found a recipe that allows him to stick around as a valuable piece of the bullpen.

YEAR	TEAM	LVL	AGE	WHIP	ERA	DRA	WARP	MPH	FB%	WHF	CSP
2017	TBA	MLB	27	1.37	4.50	4.10	1.4	93.8	44.3	11.8	48.2
2018	TBA	MLB	28	1.22	4.07	4.89	0.1	94.5	46.1	12.8	48.5
2018	ARI	MLB	28	1.89	9.00	5.20	0.0	94.0	46.1	14.3	48
2019	ARI	MLB	29	1.40	4.71	3.62	1.3	94.2	50.4	11.9	48.6
2020	ARI	MLB	30	1.23	3.78	4.01	0.9	93.4	47.1	12.3	48.3

Matt Andriese, continued

Pitch Shape vs LHH

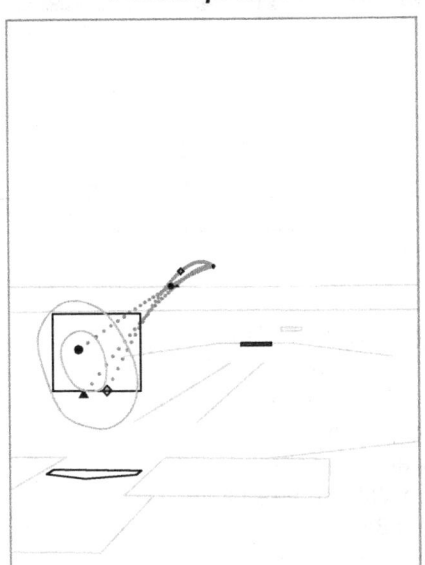

Pitch Shape vs RHH

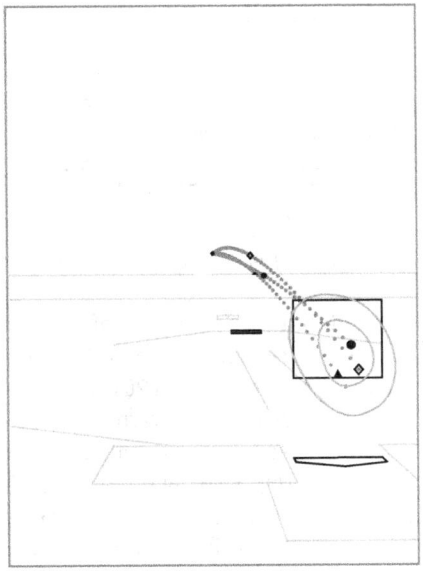

Type	Frequency	Velocity	H Movement	V Movement
● Fastball	49.7%	92.7 [101]	-5.9 [104]	-14 [105]
☐ Sinker				
+ Cutter				
▲ Changeup	37.1%	86.1 [103]	-3.5 [136]	-31.9 [87]
✕ Splitter				
▽ Slider				
◇ Curveball	11.0%	81 [108]	4.8 [89]	-47.8 [99]
✪ Slow Curveball				
✴ Knuckleball				
▼ Screwball				

Angels Player Analysis - 49

Luke Bard RHP

Born: 11/13/90 Age: 29 Bats: R Throws: R
Height: 6'3" Weight: 200 Origin: Round 1, 2012 Draft (#42 overall)

YEAR	TEAM	LVL	AGE	W	L	SV	G	GS	IP	H	HR	BB/9	K/9	K	GB%	BABIP
2017	CHT	AA	26	4	3	5	33	0	52^1	50	4	3.4	13.4	78	35%	.380
2017	ROC	AAA	26	0	0	0	8	0	13	13	1	2.8	14.5	21	30%	.400
2018	ROC	AAA	27	3	3	1	32	0	48^1	54	6	3.4	9.7	52	37%	.356
2018	LAA	MLB	27	0	0	0	8	0	11^2	10	4	3.9	10.0	13	31%	.214
2019	SLC	AAA	28	2	4	1	16	1	19	28	4	4.7	12.3	26	33%	.453
2019	LAA	MLB	28	3	3	0	32	3	49	41	8	2.4	7.3	40	37%	.248
2020	LAA	MLB	29	1	2	0	29	0	30	30	6	3.4	8.8	30	36%	.292

Comparables: B.J. Rosenberg, Luis Santos, Jose A. Valdez

More often than not, the life of a pitching prospect is filled with injury and woe. With a minor-league career full of pauses and detours since his comp-pick selection by the Twins in 2012, Bard is a living example of this principle. Despite a career of struggle, the former Rule 5 pick put together a four-game stretch in September—against the Yankees, Astros, and A's, no less—in which he retired 20 batters in a row, striking out eight of them. Will this be enough to keep him in the bullpen mix in 2020? Until we see what Bard brings to the table in the spring, this is a matter, as befits his name, for the prophets and the poets.

YEAR	TEAM	LVL	AGE	WHIP	ERA	DRA	WARP	MPH	FB%	WHF	CSP
2017	CHT	AA	26	1.34	2.58	3.89	0.6				
2017	ROC	AAA	26	1.31	3.46	3.31	0.3				
2018	ROC	AAA	27	1.49	4.66	6.05	-0.5				
2018	LAA	MLB	27	1.29	5.40	6.83	-0.3	94.5	55.4	9.9	46.1
2019	SLC	AAA	28	2.00	7.11	6.79	-0.1				
2019	LAA	MLB	28	1.10	4.78	4.81	0.3	96.1	44.1	13	47.1
2020	LAA	MLB	29	1.37	5.02	5.02	0.1	95.2	46.1	12.4	46.6

Luke Bard, continued

Pitch Shape vs LHH

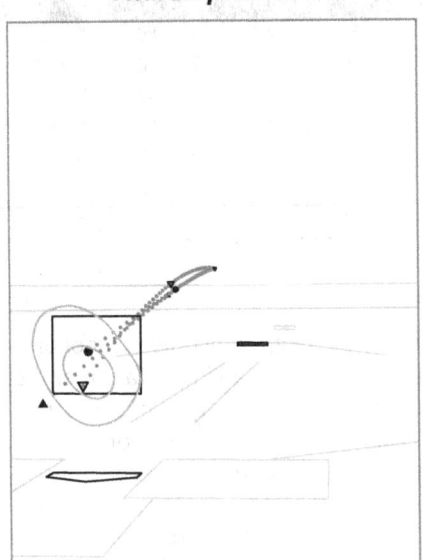

Pitch Shape vs RHH

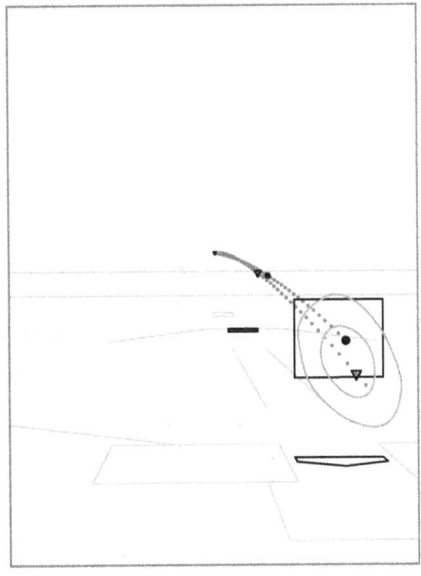

Type	Frequency	Velocity	H Movement	V Movement
● Fastball	44.1%	94.6 [106]	-9.4 [88]	-13.5 [106]
☐ Sinker				
+ Cutter				
▲ Changeup	5.4%	87.5 [108]	-14.2 [86]	-26.8 [102]
✕ Splitter				
▽ Slider	50.4%	86.3 [108]	5 [100]	-31.6 [104]
◇ Curveball				
⊕ Slow Curveball				
✳ Knuckleball				
▼ Screwball				

Jacob Barnes RHP

Born: 04/14/90 Age: 30 Bats: R Throws: R
Height: 6'2" Weight: 220 Origin: Round 14, 2011 Draft (#431 overall)

YEAR	TEAM	LVL	AGE	W	L	SV	G	GS	IP	H	HR	BB/9	K/9	K	GB%	BABIP
2017	MIL	MLB	27	3	4	2	73	0	72	57	8	4.1	10.0	80	54%	.272
2018	CSP	AAA	28	1	0	2	11	0	11^2	5	0	6.2	7.7	10	64%	.161
2018	MIL	MLB	28	0	1	2	49	0	48^2	51	4	4.3	8.7	47	51%	.329
2019	SAN	AAA	29	2	0	1	14	0	14	14	3	1.3	9.6	15	52%	.282
2019	KCA	MLB	29	0	4	0	15	0	13	14	4	7.6	6.9	10	50%	.250
2019	MIL	MLB	29	1	1	0	18	1	19^2	22	3	5.0	10.1	22	47%	.322
2020	KCA	MLB	30	2	2	0	33	0	35	31	5	3.9	9.3	36	48%	.286

Comparables: Josh Lueke, Erik Goeddel, Félix Peña

There are three easy methods to make time fly by: sleep, consume alcohol or pitch in relief. It was two scant years ago that Barnes was an important member of one of the best relief corps in the game; this fall he was making bus trips to Omaha and serving up free passes to Billy Hamilton. It made sense for the Royals to take a flier, but his fastball and slider appear to be damaged goods, and his control, never a strong suit, has grown increasingly perilous. Entering arbitration, he'll probably find himself in Triple-A next year, searching for a way to make time move backward. Unfortunately for Barnes, that's a lot harder.

YEAR	TEAM	LVL	AGE	WHIP	ERA	DRA	WARP	MPH	FB%	WHF	CSP
2017	MIL	MLB	27	1.25	4.00	3.67	1.2	99.3	54.2	16.5	41.8
2018	CSP	AAA	28	1.11	1.54	2.83	0.3				
2018	MIL	MLB	28	1.52	3.33	3.54	0.8	98.0	50.5	14.6	44.6
2019	SAN	AAA	29	1.14	4.50	2.95	0.4				
2019	KCA	MLB	29	1.92	8.31	7.18	-0.3	96.2	50.4	9.7	41
2019	MIL	MLB	29	1.68	6.86	5.54	0.0	95.9	46.4	9.4	41.9
2020	KCA	MLB	30	1.33	4.13	4.18	0.4	97.1	50.9	13.6	42.5

Jacob Barnes, continued

Pitch Shape vs LHH

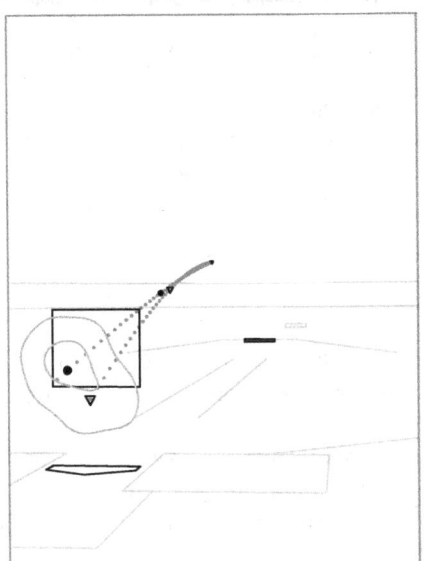

Pitch Shape vs RHH

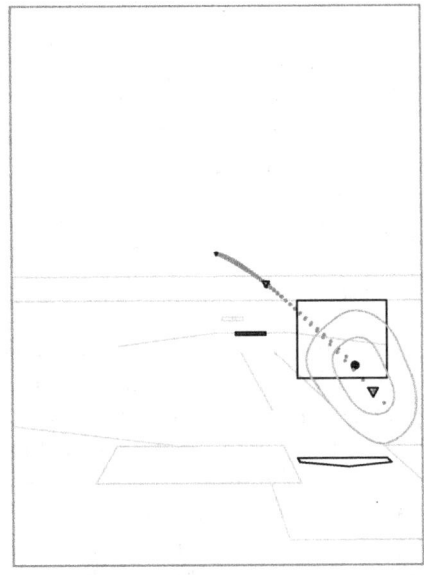

Type	Frequency	Velocity	H Movement	V Movement
● Fastball	48.0%	94.1 [105]	-1.7 [123]	-13.2 [107]
☐ Sinker				
+ Cutter				
▲ Changeup				
✕ Splitter				
▽ Slider	51.8%	88.7 [118]	4.6 [98]	-25.6 [122]
◇ Curveball				
✦ Slow Curveball				
✱ Knuckleball				
▼ Screwball				

Angels Player Analysis - 53

Los Angeles Angels 2020

Jaime Barria   RHP
Born: 07/18/96   Age: 23   Bats: R   Throws: R
Height: 6'1"   Weight: 210   Origin: International Free Agent, 2013

YEAR	TEAM	LVL	AGE	W	L	SV	G	GS	IP	H	HR	BB/9	K/9	K	GB%	BABIP
2017	INL	A+	20	4	3	0	11	11	65¹	48	6	1.8	7.9	57	35%	.236
2017	MOB	AA	20	1	6	0	12	12	61²	62	8	2.2	6.9	47	29%	.284
2017	SLC	AAA	20	2	0	0	3	3	14²	11	0	1.8	8.0	13	29%	.262
2018	SLC	AAA	21	0	0	0	5	5	18	20	2	2.5	9.5	19	28%	.353
2018	LAA	MLB	21	10	9	0	26	26	129¹	117	17	3.3	6.8	98	37%	.272
2019	SLC	AAA	22	3	3	0	10	10	48¹	73	16	1.9	8.2	44	27%	.368
2019	LAA	MLB	22	4	10	0	19	13	82²	92	24	2.9	8.2	75	36%	.287
2020	LAA	MLB	23	4	3	0	25	8	57	57	11	2.9	7.6	49	34%	.282

Comparables: Lucas Giolito, Bryse Wilson, Peter Lambert

If you have any doubts about whom the hyperball hurt in 2019, look no further than Barria. Over the last two seasons, Barria has been more or less the same pitcher in terms of pitch mix and velocity: he's a slider/four-seam guy whose fastball is accurate but pretty straight and eminently hittable. In 2018, this made him a fringy-but-usable piece at the end of the rotation. In 2019, it made him a batting practice tosser who was saved only by the existence of the Orioles' David Hess from leading the HR/9 charts for pitchers with at least 80 innings. Barria, more than most, will be eager to see what the primary tool of his trade looks, feels, and plays like in 2020.

YEAR	TEAM	LVL	AGE	WHIP	ERA	DRA	WARP	MPH	FB%	WHF	CSP
2017	INL	A+	20	0.93	2.48	2.54	2.1				
2017	MOB	AA	20	1.25	3.21	5.23	0.0				
2017	SLC	AAA	20	0.95	2.45	2.89	0.5				
2018	SLC	AAA	21	1.39	3.50	4.84	0.1				
2018	LAA	MLB	21	1.27	3.41	5.67	-0.5	93.2	49.6	11.2	45
2019	SLC	AAA	22	1.72	9.68	7.27	-0.3				
2019	LAA	MLB	22	1.44	6.42	7.74	-1.9	93.3	36.9	9.8	47.2
2020	LAA	MLB	23	1.33	4.71	4.85	0.4	93.2	45.3	10.9	47.9

Jaime Barria, continued

Pitch Shape vs LHH

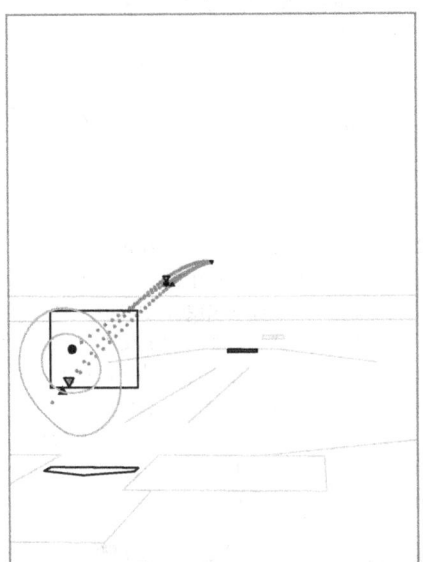

Pitch Shape vs RHH

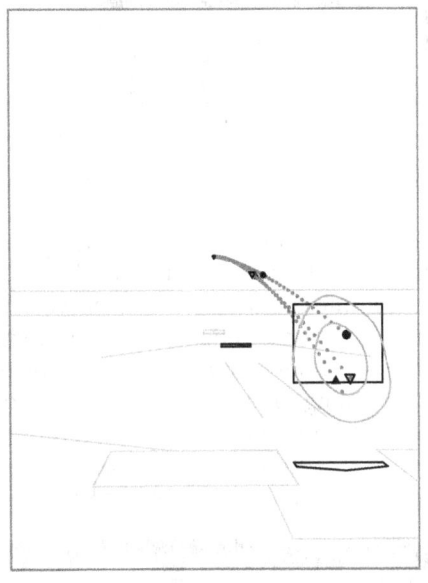

Type	Frequency	Velocity	H Movement	V Movement
● Fastball	33.8%	91.8 [98]	-5.1 [108]	-13.8 [106]
☐ Sinker	3.1%	92.2 [98]	-11.1 [110]	-16 [115]
+ Cutter				
▲ Changeup	16.4%	83.4 [93]	-10 [105]	-27.4 [100]
✕ Splitter				
▽ Slider	46.1%	84.1 [99]	3.2 [93]	-29.6 [110]
◇ Curveball				
⊕ Slow Curveball				
✳ Knuckleball				
▼ Screwball				

Angels Player Analysis - 55

Los Angeles Angels 2020

Cam Bedrosian RHP
Born: 10/02/91 Age: 28 Bats: R Throws: R
Height: 6'1" Weight: 225 Origin: Round 1, 2010 Draft (#29 overall)

YEAR	TEAM	LVL	AGE	W	L	SV	G	GS	IP	H	HR	BB/9	K/9	K	GB%	BABIP
2017	LAA	MLB	25	6	5	6	48	0	44^2	41	5	3.4	10.7	53	45%	.313
2018	LAA	MLB	26	5	4	1	71	0	64	63	7	3.7	8.0	57	50%	.315
2019	LAA	MLB	27	3	3	1	59	7	61^1	48	7	3.2	9.4	64	48%	.253
2020	LAA	MLB	28	3	3	0	52	0	55	52	8	3.8	9.3	56	48%	.296

Comparables: Arodys Vizcaíno, Chris Perez, Dominic Leone

Despite its ending with the always-ominous "forearm strain" diagnosis, Bedrosian's 2019 was far from a failure. Though his 2017 occupation of the closer throne was a brief one, he was more valuable to the Angels in both late-inning and occasional opener roles this past season. Even as his fastball has steadily, if slowly, declined into the high end of the low 90s, his slider is still devastating, with a down-and-in drop that makes him even more effective against lefties than same-sided hitters. If healthy, Bedrosian looks to be back in the high-leverage mix again, with a return to closing royalty unlikely, but, given the rabble of pretenders in the Halos' pen, not impossible.

YEAR	TEAM	LVL	AGE	WHIP	ERA	DRA	WARP	MPH	FB%	WHF	CSP
2017	LAA	MLB	25	1.30	4.43	2.97	1.1	95.8	57.7	13.5	46.5
2018	LAA	MLB	26	1.39	3.80	4.21	0.5	95.6	55.5	8.6	47.9
2019	LAA	MLB	27	1.14	3.23	3.50	1.3	94.7	47.8	13.2	45.9
2020	LAA	MLB	28	1.36	4.32	4.36	0.5	94.7	52.9	11.7	47

Cam Bedrosian, continued

Pitch Shape vs LHH

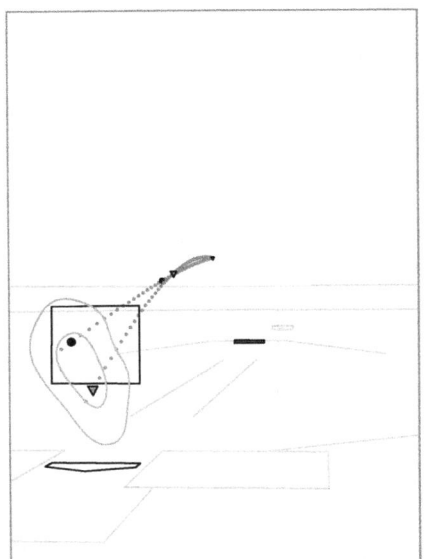

Pitch Shape vs RHH

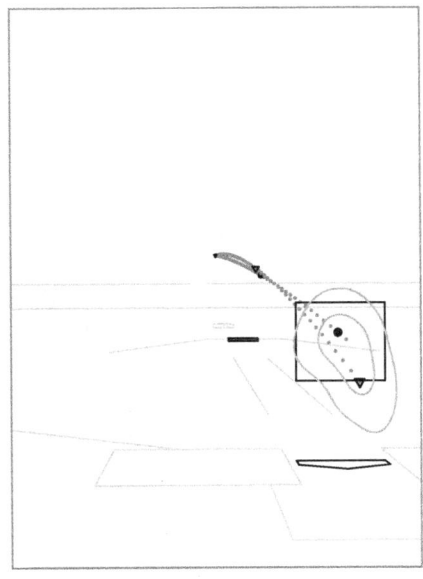

Type	Frequency	Velocity	H Movement	V Movement
● Fastball	47.8%	93.4 [103]	-1.8 [122]	-12.8 [108]
☐ Sinker				
+ Cutter				
▲ Changeup				
✕ Splitter				
▽ Slider	50.9%	83.6 [97]	4.2 [97]	-39.1 [83]
◇ Curveball				
⊕ Slow Curveball				
✷ Knuckleball				
▼ Screwball				

Los Angeles Angels 2020

Dylan Bundy   RHP
Born: 11/15/92   Age: 27   Bats: B   Throws: R
Height: 6'1"   Weight: 200   Origin: Round 1, 2011 Draft (#4 overall)

YEAR	TEAM	LVL	AGE	W	L	SV	G	GS	IP	H	HR	BB/9	K/9	K	GB%	BABIP
2017	BAL	MLB	24	13	9	0	28	28	169^2	152	26	2.7	8.1	152	33%	.273
2018	BAL	MLB	25	8	16	0	31	31	171^2	188	41	2.8	9.6	184	35%	.316
2019	BAL	MLB	26	7	14	0	30	30	161^2	161	29	3.2	9.0	162	42%	.297
2020	LAA	MLB	27	10	8	0	26	26	137	131	26	3.3	9.1	139	39%	.287

Comparables: Chad Kuhl, Robert Gsellman, A.J. Cole

In the fifth inning of his May 11 start against the Los Angeles Angels, Bundy got a visit from pitching coach Doug Brocail asking if he was hurt. The one-time flamethrower wasn't even hitting 90 mph anymore, and it's not like the fastball he's carried the last few years was much better. From the start of 2017 until that day, Bundy allowed a league-high 45 home runs on his fastball. But that start was enough to wean himself off of it, and his higher frequency of secondary pitches made for…pretty much more of the same, except fewer home runs. On its day, Bundy's slider is still a swing-and-miss pitch. He grew more comfortable pitching with his curveball and changeup, and worked more on locating his fastball at the edges. The resulting pitcher was league-average in 2019, and a full transformation into the type of junk-baller he started to become might only slightly improve that going forward.

YEAR	TEAM	LVL	AGE	WHIP	ERA	DRA	WARP	MPH	FB%	WHF	CSP
2017	BAL	MLB	24	1.20	4.24	4.93	1.2	94.4	53.8	12.3	46.4
2018	BAL	MLB	25	1.41	5.45	5.34	-0.1	93.7	55.8	13.5	50.2
2019	BAL	MLB	26	1.35	4.79	4.88	1.6	93.4	50	13.8	46.8
2020	LAA	MLB	27	1.32	4.57	4.67	1.4	93.3	53.6	13.5	48.4

Dylan Bundy, continued

Pitch Shape vs LHH

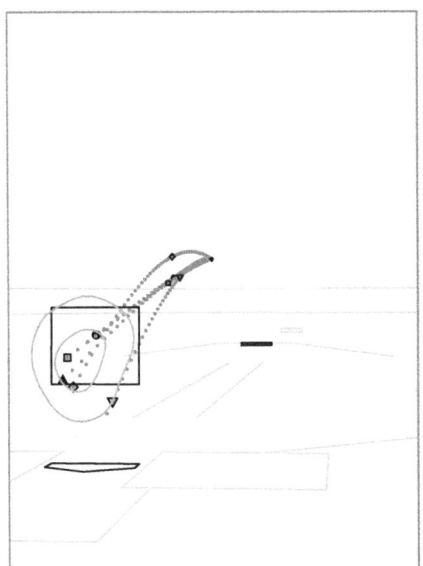

Pitch Shape vs RHH

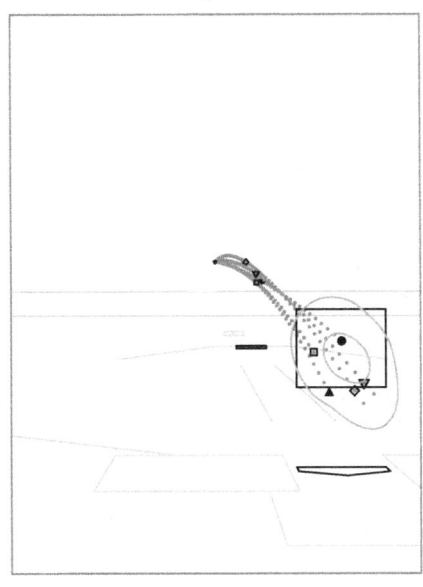

Type	Frequency	Velocity	H Movement	V Movement
● Fastball	42.6%	91.6 [98]	-4.3 [111]	-12.8 [108]
☐ Sinker	7.4%	91.7 [95]	-11.5 [107]	-16.5 [114]
+ Cutter				
▲ Changeup	17.3%	83.9 [95]	-10.8 [102]	-28.2 [98]
✕ Splitter				
▽ Slider	22.8%	81.5 [88]	4.5 [98]	-38.2 [85]
◇ Curveball	9.9%	75.3 [89]	8 [102]	-55.5 [83]
⊕ Slow Curveball				
✱ Knuckleball				
▼ Screwball				

Los Angeles Angels 2020

Ty Buttrey   RHP
Born: 03/31/93   Age: 27   Bats: L   Throws: R
Height: 6'6"   Weight: 240   Origin: Round 4, 2012 Draft (#151 overall)

YEAR	TEAM	LVL	AGE	W	L	SV	G	GS	IP	H	HR	BB/9	K/9	K	GB%	BABIP
2017	PME	AA	24	1	4	4	30	0	46	39	1	4.5	11.0	56	50%	.339
2017	PAW	AAA	24	1	1	0	10	0	17^2	21	2	5.1	9.2	18	53%	.358
2018	PAW	AAA	25	1	1	1	32	0	44	36	4	2.9	13.1	64	45%	.320
2018	LAA	MLB	25	0	1	4	16	0	16^1	15	0	2.8	11.0	20	58%	.333
2019	LAA	MLB	26	6	7	2	72	0	72^1	69	8	2.9	10.5	84	45%	.323
2020	LAA	MLB	27	3	3	9	63	0	67	62	9	3.3	10.3	77	46%	.308

Comparables: Marcus Hatley, Victor Alcántara, Dovydas Neverauskas

There was a minor scandal at the MLB offices in the midsummer of 2019. The league was approving nicknames for the Players' Weekend jerseys, and there was a mysterious text from the 714 area code. All it contained was two emojis: a peach, and a tree.
"Peachtree?" The confused intern who received the text looked perplexed. "Who is that?"
Over the intern's shoulder, another intern chimed in.
"It's not a peach. It's…a butt."
"Butt … tree … Butt-tree. I GET IT. Ty Buttrey! Could've sworn he was gonna go with some kind of 'butter' pun, but OK." There was a pause. "Wait, so you're telling me that we get our panties in a bunch about bat flips but we're OK having an icon of, well … a human ass … on our jerseys? I mean, who is Buttrey, anyway?"
The other intern sighed. "Big body reliever. Red Sox draft pick, went to the Angels in the Ian Kinsler trade, good heat, killer change, really cut down on his walks the last couple of years. Good pitcher. Bit unlucky in 2019, or he could've been the closer instead of Robles."
"No, I *knew* that. I meant, who does he *think* he is? Listen, I knew Box Burger. And Butt Tree is *no* Box Burger."

YEAR	TEAM	LVL	AGE	WHIP	ERA	DRA	WARP	MPH	FB%	WHF	CSP
2017	PME	AA	24	1.35	3.72	3.58	0.7				
2017	PAW	AAA	24	1.75	7.64	6.68	-0.3				
2018	PAW	AAA	25	1.14	2.25	3.06	1.0				
2018	LAA	MLB	25	1.22	3.31	2.90	0.4	98.6	58	14	47.3
2019	LAA	MLB	26	1.27	3.98	3.54	1.4	99.1	57.2	12.7	50.2
2020	LAA	MLB	27	1.29	3.95	4.10	0.8	98.5	58	13.1	49.5

Ty Buttrey, continued

Pitch Shape vs LHH

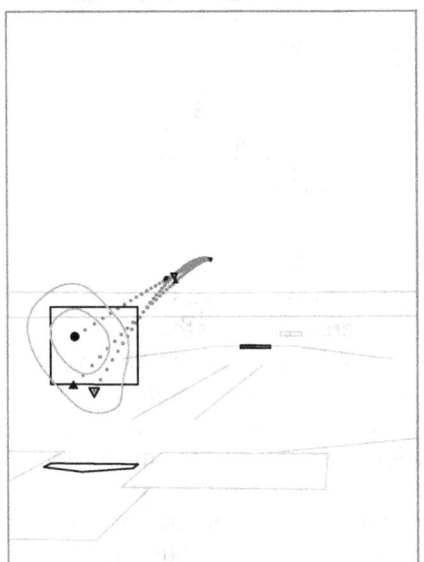

Pitch Shape vs RHH

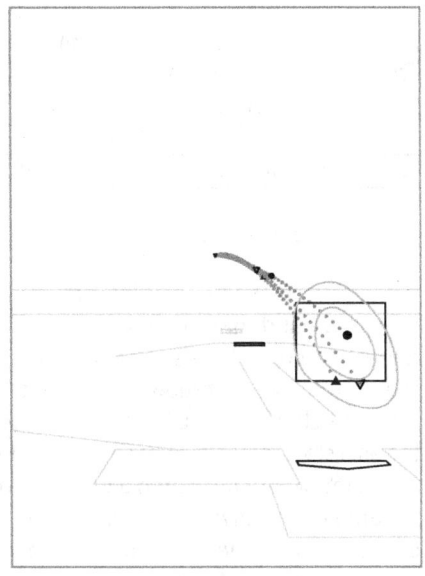

Type	Frequency	Velocity	H Movement	V Movement
● Fastball	57.1%	97.4 [114]	-10.7 [83]	-13.5 [106]
☐ Sinker				
+ Cutter				
▲ Changeup	13.3%	87.9 [110]	-14.7 [83]	-28.4 [97]
✕ Splitter				
▽ Slider	29.5%	84 [99]	2.6 [90]	-36.8 [89]
◇ Curveball				
⊕ Slow Curveball				
✳ Knuckleball				
▼ Screwball				

Los Angeles Angels 2020

Trevor Cahill RHP
Born: 03/01/88   Age: 32   Bats: R   Throws: R
Height: 6'4"   Weight: 230   Origin: Round 2, 2006 Draft (#66 overall)

YEAR	TEAM	LVL	AGE	W	L	SV	G	GS	IP	H	HR	BB/9	K/9	K	GB%	BABIP
2017	SDN	MLB	29	4	3	0	11	11	61	58	6	3.5	10.6	72	58%	.329
2017	KCA	MLB	29	0	0	0	10	3	23	33	10	8.2	5.9	15	54%	.319
2018	NAS	AAA	30	0	1	0	3	3	13^2	7	0	5.3	11.2	17	81%	.226
2018	OAK	MLB	30	7	4	0	21	20	110	90	8	3.4	8.2	100	54%	.278
2019	LAA	MLB	31	4	9	0	37	11	102^1	111	25	3.4	7.1	81	46%	.283
2020	LAA	MLB	32	2	2	0	33	0	35	33	5	3.8	7.8	30	49%	.283

Comparables: Jair Jurrjens, Jhoulys Chacín, Chris Volstad

While cats, as the myth holds, are afforded nine lives, pitchers seldom get more than one—and that's if they're lucky. Cahill's career has nonetheless taken a feline trajectory: His rise as a dependable ground-baller with the A's and Diamondbacks eventually stalled out, leaving him an itinerant reliever with five different clubs from 2015 to 2017. It took a return to Oakland to resuscitate his life as a starter, but his East Bay rejuvenation was subsequently squandered in Anaheim, where he signed a one-year deal. The sinker, his stock in trade, became the pitch *non grata* in the age of uppercutting hitters and the, ah ... enhanced offensive environment, and Cahill found himself in bullpen and bulk-pitcher purgatory by June. Cats have a preternatural ability to land on their feet; Cahill will have to make some fairly acrobatic contortions to do the same with a major-league staff in 2020.

YEAR	TEAM	LVL	AGE	WHIP	ERA	DRA	WARP	MPH	FB%	WHF	CSP
2017	SDN	MLB	29	1.34	3.69	3.51	1.4	93.5	45.7	13.4	42.4
2017	KCA	MLB	29	2.35	8.22	6.61	-0.3	93.8	50	7.3	41.7
2018	NAS	AAA	30	1.10	2.63	2.59	0.5				
2018	OAK	MLB	30	1.19	3.76	3.48	2.3	94.4	41.1	12.1	44.5
2019	LAA	MLB	31	1.47	5.98	5.97	-0.4	93.7	36.5	10.8	47.7
2020	LAA	MLB	32	1.38	4.48	4.54	0.2	93.0	40.1	11.3	44.8

Trevor Cahill, continued

Pitch Shape vs LHH

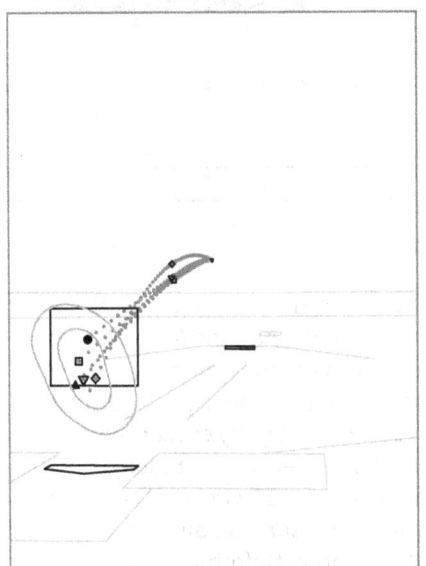

Pitch Shape vs RHH

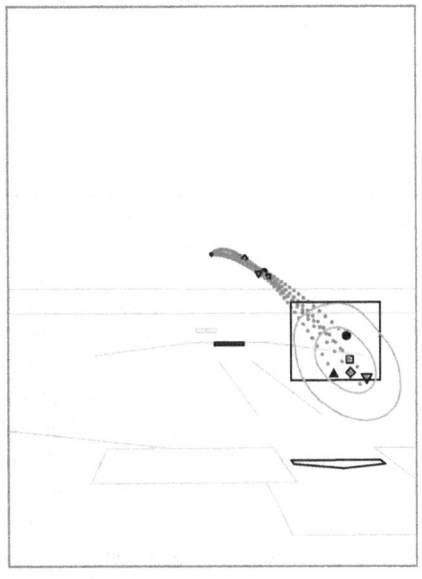

Type	Frequency	Velocity	H Movement	V Movement
● Fastball	8.4%	92.5 [100]	-8.3 [94]	-16.4 [99]
◻ Sinker	28.0%	92.1 [97]	-13.8 [92]	-22.2 [94]
+ Cutter				
▲ Changeup	23.3%	83.8 [95]	-11.6 [98]	-33.7 [81]
✕ Splitter				
▽ Slider	18.2%	86.1 [107]	1.1 [84]	-29 [112]
◇ Curveball	21.8%	79.9 [104]	10.6 [112]	-48.8 [97]
✣ Slow Curveball				
✳ Knuckleball				
▼ Screwball				

Angels Player Analysis - 63

Griffin Canning RHP

Born: 05/11/96 Age: 24 Bats: R Throws: R
Height: 6'2" Weight: 180 Origin: Round 2, 2017 Draft (#47 overall)

YEAR	TEAM	LVL	AGE	W	L	SV	G	GS	IP	H	HR	BB/9	K/9	K	GB%	BABIP
2018	INL	A+	22	0	0	0	2	2	8²	4	0	3.1	12.5	12	56%	.222
2018	MOB	AA	22	1	0	0	10	10	45²	27	2	3.7	9.7	49	48%	.229
2018	SLC	AAA	22	3	3	0	13	13	59	68	6	3.4	9.8	64	42%	.376
2019	SLC	AAA	23	1	0	0	3	3	16	13	0	1.1	9.6	17	42%	.317
2019	LAA	MLB	23	5	6	0	18	17	90¹	80	14	3.0	9.6	96	39%	.280
2020	LAA	MLB	24	9	6	0	23	23	120	103	18	3.4	9.8	131	39%	.279

Comparables: Kevin Gausman, Zack Wheeler, Dylan Cease

With the untimely UCL injury to Shohei Ohtani and the inevitable ailment perpetually lurking around the corner for Andrew Heaney, the Angels have to walk a fine line with Canning, their most promising home-grown arm in years. On the one hand, it would make sense—especially given his injury history in both college and the minors—to keep him gently but tightly ensconced in bubble wrap in a climate-controlled safe room, the seal to be broken only when the time of contention arrives. On the other hand, the 23-year-old was plenty ready when the rotation sprung several leaks in midsummer and proved himself a worthy mid-rotation arm, with the upside for more. Unfortunately, with an air of inevitability, the dreaded "elbow inflammation" sidelined the promising rookie for the rest of the season, and health, more than ability, will be his primary question mark going forward.

YEAR	TEAM	LVL	AGE	WHIP	ERA	DRA	WARP	MPH	FB%	WHF	CSP
2018	INL	A+	22	0.81	0.00	2.44	0.3				
2018	MOB	AA	22	1.01	1.97	2.75	1.4				
2018	SLC	AAA	22	1.53	5.49	4.78	0.5				
2019	SLC	AAA	23	0.94	0.56	2.06	0.7				
2019	LAA	MLB	23	1.22	4.58	4.50	1.2	95.8	42.1	14.6	44.5
2020	LAA	MLB	24	1.24	3.81	3.98	2.1	95.6	43.3	15.1	45.8

Griffin Canning, continued

Pitch Shape vs LHH

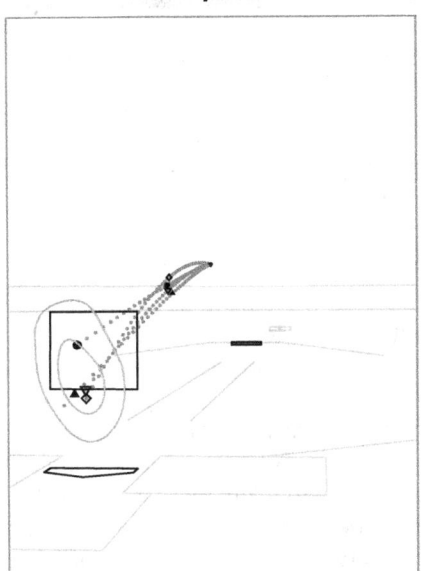

Pitch Shape vs RHH

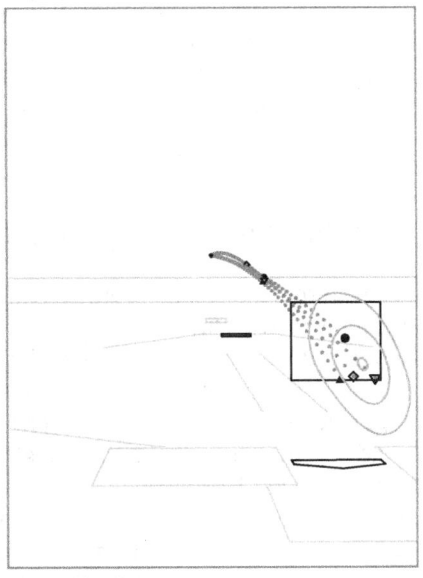

Type	Frequency	Velocity	H Movement	V Movement
● Fastball	42.1%	94.2 [105]	-7.6 [97]	-12.5 [109]
☐ Sinker				
+ Cutter				
▲ Changeup	12.7%	89.4 [115]	-12.7 [93]	-23.1 [113]
✕ Splitter				
▽ Slider	29.2%	89.2 [120]	2 [87]	-24.9 [124]
◇ Curveball	16.0%	82.4 [112]	8.4 [104]	-41.4 [113]
⊕ Slow Curveball				
✱ Knuckleball				
▼ Screwball				

Los Angeles Angels 2020

Taylor Cole RHP

Born: 08/20/89 Age: 30 Bats: R Throws: R
Height: 6'1" Weight: 200 Origin: Round 29, 2011 Draft (#889 overall)

YEAR	TEAM	LVL	AGE	W	L	SV	G	GS	IP	H	HR	BB/9	K/9	K	GB%	BABIP
2017	TOR	MLB	27	0	0	0	1	0	1	6	0	9.0	9.0	1	57%	.857
2018	SLC	AAA	28	3	0	6	34	0	55^1	55	6	4.4	10.6	65	48%	.343
2018	LAA	MLB	28	4	2	0	18	2	36	20	3	3.0	9.8	39	52%	.218
2019	SLC	AAA	29	3	0	3	16	0	20^2	29	5	2.6	10.5	24	35%	.414
2019	LAA	MLB	29	3	4	0	38	6	51^2	58	2	4.2	8.7	50	48%	.366
2020	LAA	MLB	30	2	2	0	40	0	43	38	5	3.7	9.2	44	46%	.290

Comparables: Félix Peña, Darin Downs, Josh Ravin

In an alternate universe, "Cole Taylor" is a similarly anonymous pitcher as the pitcher whose profile you are reading—but "Cole Taylor" throws lefty instead of righty, and he's a bullpen piece for, let's say, the Reds. We could easily slip in a capsule, or at the very least a lineout, about this entirely-made-up doppelgänger. We could talk about his fringy arsenal, muse about how if he could fine-tune his command he might get some high-leverage looks, point out how it's players like him who should be especially thankful for that 26th roster spot next season. And we would be willing to bet that precisely none of you, not even the most rabid Reds fans, would write in to our editors and complain that we inserted an entirely fictitious pitcher into the book. Just like none of you probably knew who "Taylor Cole" was before his two-inning start of a combined no-hitter with Félix Peña in July. His part in a historic game saves Cole from oblivion, but it remains to be seen if it can save his job as a major-league reliever.

YEAR	TEAM	LVL	AGE	WHIP	ERA	DRA	WARP	MPH	FB%	WHF	CSP
2017	TOR	MLB	27	7.00	36.00	11.11	-0.1	95.8	58.5	9.8	43.2
2018	SLC	AAA	28	1.48	5.37	4.02	0.7				
2018	LAA	MLB	28	0.89	2.75	4.24	0.3	95.3	41	15.9	41.8
2019	SLC	AAA	29	1.69	5.23	5.30	0.2				
2019	LAA	MLB	29	1.59	5.92	5.09	0.2	95.6	42.2	12.4	44
2020	LAA	MLB	30	1.30	3.81	3.92	0.6	94.7	41.9	13.5	42.9

Taylor Cole, continued

Pitch Shape vs LHH

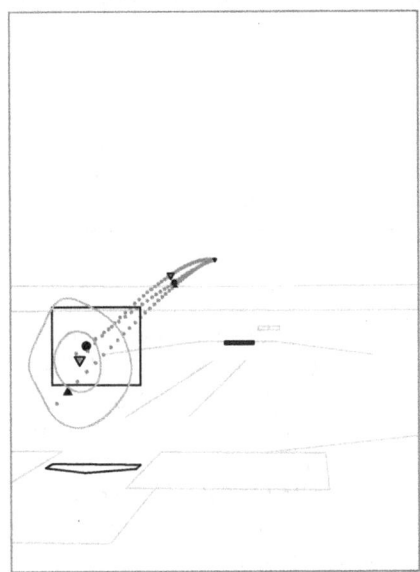

Pitch Shape vs RHH

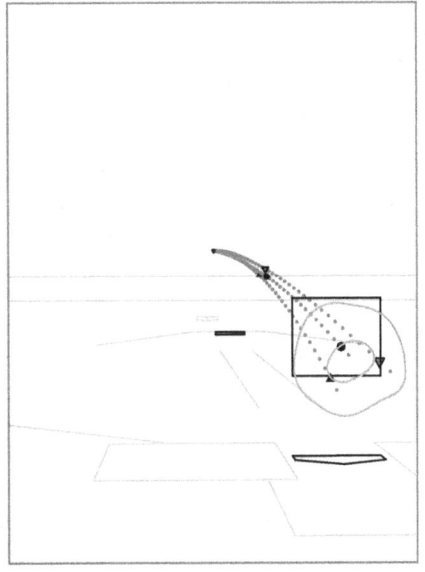

Type	Frequency	Velocity	H Movement	V Movement
● Fastball	42.2%	93.4 [103]	-10.4 [84]	-14.2 [104]
☐ Sinker				
+ Cutter				
▲ Changeup	31.4%	87.2 [107]	-12.8 [92]	-27.1 [101]
✕ Splitter				
▽ Slider	24.3%	87.3 [112]	2.4 [89]	-27.1 [117]
◇ Curveball				
⬥ Slow Curveball				
✳ Knuckleball				
▼ Screwball				

Andrew Heaney LHP

Born: 06/05/91 Age: 29 Bats: L Throws: L
Height: 6'2" Weight: 200 Origin: Round 1, 2012 Draft (#9 overall)

YEAR	TEAM	LVL	AGE	W	L	SV	G	GS	IP	H	HR	BB/9	K/9	K	GB%	BABIP
2017	ANG	RK	26	0	1	0	3	3	10^1	11	0	0.9	13.1	15	42%	.423
2017	SLC	AAA	26	1	1	0	3	3	17^1	17	2	2.1	7.3	14	39%	.306
2017	LAA	MLB	26	1	2	0	5	5	21^2	27	12	3.7	11.2	27	34%	.283
2018	INL	A+	27	1	0	0	1	1	6^1	2	0	1.4	8.5	6	73%	.133
2018	LAA	MLB	27	9	10	0	30	30	180	171	27	2.2	9.0	180	44%	.294
2019	LAA	MLB	28	4	6	0	18	18	95^1	93	20	2.8	11.1	118	34%	.312
2020	LAA	MLB	29	10	7	0	26	26	137	131	26	2.8	10.3	158	37%	.302

Comparables: Steven Matz, Wade LeBlanc, Jerad Eickhoff

Like a showy sports car notorious for mechanical breakdowns, Heaney looks and feels great on the road—but only for short stretches and always with the looming dread that a breakdown is just around the next bend. In 2018, he ran smoothly the entire year and showed the kind of performance that could land him near the top of a competitive team's rotation. But 2019 was more trouble under the hood, and even though he revved higher (to the tune of 11 strikeouts per nine), his shoulder couldn't take the redlining and he went back to the garage with shoulder inflammation in July. A late-season return showed him in need of a tune-up, and 2020 leaves the Angels happy to have him in the fleet, but sorely in need of more reliable vehicles to get them anywhere near the postseason.

YEAR	TEAM	LVL	AGE	WHIP	ERA	DRA	WARP	MPH	FB%	WHF	CSP
2017	ANG	RK	26	1.16	1.74	2.46	0.4				
2017	SLC	AAA	26	1.21	3.12	4.42	0.2				
2017	LAA	MLB	26	1.66	7.06	5.71	0.0	94.5	61.6	14.6	44.5
2018	INL	A+	27	0.47	1.42	2.33	0.2				
2018	LAA	MLB	27	1.20	4.15	3.63	3.5	94.6	58.1	12.7	50.8
2019	LAA	MLB	28	1.29	4.91	5.31	0.5	94.7	58	15.2	49.6
2020	LAA	MLB	29	1.26	4.29	4.44	1.7	94.0	58.3	13.8	48.7

Andrew Heaney, continued

Pitch Shape vs LHH

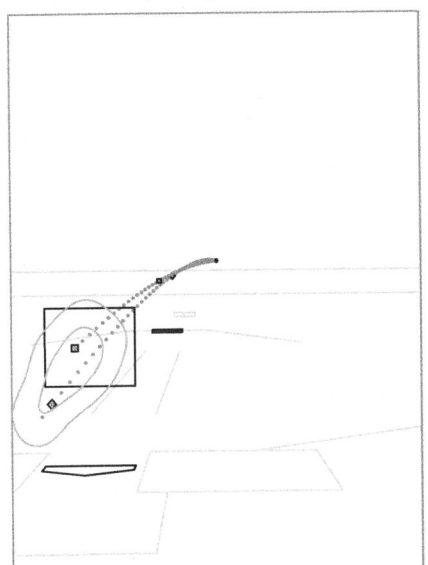

Pitch Shape vs RHH

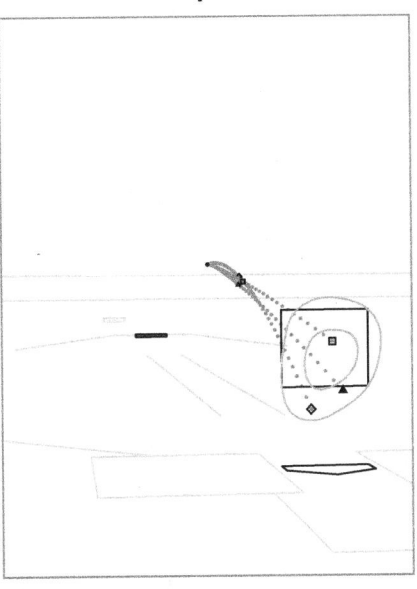

Type	Frequency	Velocity	H Movement	V Movement
● Fastball				
☐ Sinker	58.0%	92.7 [100]	12.8 [99]	-14.9 [119]
+ Cutter				
▲ Changeup	15.0%	84.8 [98]	15.5 [80]	-27.3 [100]
✕ Splitter				
▽ Slider				
◇ Curveball	27.0%	79.5 [103]	-5.6 [93]	-42.7 [110]
⊕ Slow Curveball				
✹ Knuckleball				
▼ Screwball				

Los Angeles Angels 2020

Dillon Peters LHP

Born: 08/31/92 Age: 27 Bats: L Throws: L
Height: 5'11" Weight: 190 Origin: Round 10, 2014 Draft (#287 overall)

YEAR	TEAM	LVL	AGE	W	L	SV	G	GS	IP	H	HR	BB/9	K/9	K	GB%	BABIP
2017	MRL	RK	24	0	1	0	2	2	6^2	3	0	5.4	8.1	6	65%	.176
2017	JUP	A+	24	1	0	0	2	2	10^2	5	0	1.7	7.6	9	59%	.185
2017	JAX	AA	24	6	2	0	9	9	45^2	33	1	2.2	7.9	40	46%	.258
2017	MIA	MLB	24	1	2	0	6	6	31^1	32	3	5.5	7.8	27	63%	.330
2018	NWO	AAA	25	6	7	0	19	19	102^2	129	15	2.5	7.5	85	46%	.355
2018	MIA	MLB	25	2	2	0	7	5	27^2	34	4	4.9	5.5	17	45%	.326
2019	SLC	AAA	26	4	1	0	13	11	57	74	11	2.7	8.7	55	50%	.366
2019	LAA	MLB	26	4	4	0	17	12	72	85	18	3.2	6.9	55	41%	.300
2020	LAA	MLB	27	2	2	0	16	5	34	37	6	3.3	6.9	26	44%	.296

Comparables: Erick Fedde, Jarlin García, Andrew Miller

This is a hypothesis that calls for empirical verification, but "Dylans" seem to come from the coasts while "Dillons" feel like they're more often found in the nation's interior. The lefty from Indianapolis confirms these hunches, though he has spent his major-league time bi-coastally: first in Miami, and now Anaheim. While offering a rotation tourniquet for the Halos late in the season, Peters showed that his fragile pitch-mix Jenga depends upon the structural stability of his changeup. Take that away, and the blocks fall quickly. Unfortunately for Peters, any 2020 plan that involves "trying to win" likely pushes him out of contention for a rotation spot on the Angels, or any playoff-credible team.

YEAR	TEAM	LVL	AGE	WHIP	ERA	DRA	WARP	MPH	FB%	WHF	CSP
2017	MRL	RK	24	1.05	1.35	3.05	0.2				
2017	JUP	A+	24	0.66	0.00	2.60	0.3				
2017	JAX	AA	24	0.96	1.97	3.11	1.1				
2017	MIA	MLB	24	1.63	5.17	3.98	0.6	93.6	49.9	10.8	44.5
2018	NWO	AAA	25	1.54	5.61	6.44	-1.0				
2018	MIA	MLB	25	1.77	7.16	5.69	-0.1	93.1	52.2	7.8	50.2
2019	SLC	AAA	26	1.60	6.47	4.72	1.1				
2019	LAA	MLB	26	1.54	5.38	7.68	-1.6	92.7	50.4	9.6	47
2020	LAA	MLB	27	1.45	5.37	5.33	0.0	92.5	51.3	9.5	48

Dillon Peters, continued

Pitch Shape vs LHH

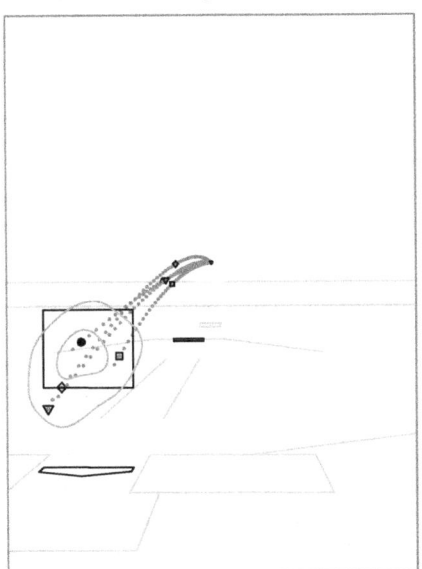

Pitch Shape vs RHH

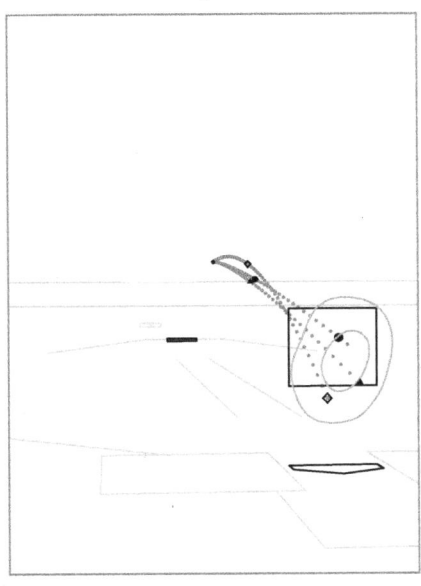

Type		Frequency	Velocity	H Movement	V Movement
●	Fastball	46.0%	91.1 [96]	4 [113]	-14.7 [103]
□	Sinker	4.4%	91 [92]	11 [111]	-18.2 [108]
+	Cutter				
▲	Changeup	21.0%	84.1 [96]	11.2 [100]	-26 [104]
✕	Splitter				
▽	Slider	4.6%	82.5 [92]	-2.3 [89]	-38.8 [84]
◇	Curveball	24.0%	76.7 [94]	-8.7 [105]	-52.6 [89]
✦	Slow Curveball				
✱	Knuckleball				
▼	Screwball				

Los Angeles Angels 2020

Félix Peña RHP
Born: 02/25/90   Age: 30   Bats: R   Throws: R
Height: 6'2"   Weight: 220   Origin: International Free Agent, 2009

YEAR	TEAM	LVL	AGE	W	L	SV	G	GS	IP	H	HR	BB/9	K/9	K	GB%	BABIP
2017	IOW	AAA	27	2	1	6	24	0	39	42	6	3.2	10.6	46	42%	.346
2017	CHN	MLB	27	1	0	0	25	0	34^1	35	8	4.7	9.7	37	35%	.300
2018	SLC	AAA	28	1	2	0	10	9	33^1	30	2	4.3	10.3	38	39%	.346
2018	LAA	MLB	28	3	5	0	19	17	92^2	87	12	2.7	8.3	85	44%	.288
2019	LAA	MLB	29	8	3	0	22	7	96^1	80	16	3.2	9.4	101	45%	.256
2020	LAA	MLB	30	3	2	0	28	5	46	42	7	3.4	9.3	48	43%	.286

Comparables: Jacob Barnes, Josh Lueke, Paul Sewald

By WARP, Peña was the 108th most valuable pitcher in the majors in 2019. By WARP, Peña was the, uh, *first* most valuable pitcher on the Angels in 2019—and this while missing the final two months of the season after tearing his ACL. He gets by on a sinker-slider combo mainly because of the filthiness of the latter, though he shouldn't be seeing lineups a third time through. Peña's true talent is probably somewhere near the midpoint of two consecutive outings in July: In the first, he gave up a solitary walk to the Mariners over seven relief innings of a combined no-hitter in the first home game following the death of teammate Tyler Skaggs; in the next, he was chased in the fifth after giving up eight runs to the Astros. In other words, he's a better-than-average pitcher whose ideal role is near the back end of a competing team's rotation.

YEAR	TEAM	LVL	AGE	WHIP	ERA	DRA	WARP	MPH	FB%	WHF	CSP
2017	IOW	AAA	27	1.44	5.54	4.47	0.4				
2017	CHN	MLB	27	1.54	5.24	5.46	-0.1	96.3	65.8	13.4	46.7
2018	SLC	AAA	28	1.38	3.51	3.84	0.6				
2018	LAA	MLB	28	1.24	4.18	4.15	1.2	94.5	57.9	11.8	46.2
2019	LAA	MLB	29	1.18	4.58	4.11	1.4	94.0	49.2	13.2	46.3
2020	LAA	MLB	30	1.29	4.22	4.34	0.5	93.7	54.2	12.7	46.2

Félix Peña, continued

Pitch Shape vs LHH

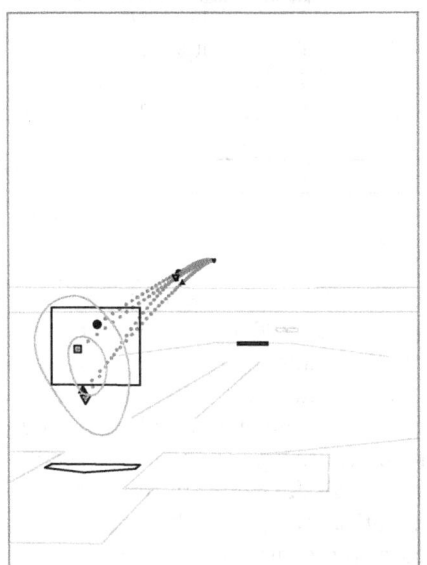

Pitch Shape vs RHH

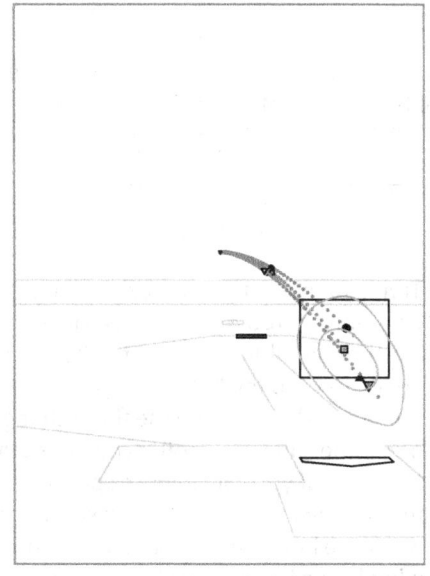

Type	Frequency	Velocity	H Movement	V Movement
● Fastball	7.1%	91.6 [98]	-9.4 [89]	-16.5 [98]
☐ Sinker	42.1%	92 [97]	-14 [91]	-19.7 [103]
+ Cutter				
▲ Changeup	11.4%	84.3 [97]	-11.4 [99]	-25.6 [105]
✕ Splitter				
▽ Slider	39.4%	82.9 [94]	2 [87]	-35.5 [93]
◇ Curveball				
✥ Slow Curveball				
✱ Knuckleball				
▼ Screwball				

Los Angeles Angels 2020

Noé Ramirez RHP
Born: 12/22/89 Age: 30 Bats: R Throws: R
Height: 6'3" Weight: 205 Origin: Round 4, 2011 Draft (#142 overall)

YEAR	TEAM	LVL	AGE	W	L	SV	G	GS	IP	H	HR	BB/9	K/9	K	GB%	BABIP
2017	PAW	AAA	27	3	3	5	33	0	48^2	40	7	3.0	10.5	57	35%	.284
2017	LAA	MLB	27	0	0	0	10	0	8^1	3	0	4.3	10.8	10	65%	.176
2017	BOS	MLB	27	0	0	0	2	0	4^2	3	2	1.9	7.7	4	23%	.091
2018	LAA	MLB	28	7	5	1	69	1	83^1	75	15	3.2	10.3	95	44%	.290
2019	LAA	MLB	29	5	4	0	51	7	67^2	59	9	2.7	10.5	79	38%	.299
2020	LAA	MLB	30	3	3	0	52	0	55	49	10	3.1	10.4	63	37%	.287

Comparables: Heath Hembree, Michael Mariot, Juan Minaya

Trying to match up Ramirez's stat line with his pitches is something of a conundrum. You'd think that a sinker barely scraping 90 mph, thrown nearly half the time, wouldn't set up a pitcher for either a double-digit K/9 nor, in 2019, an ability to keep the ball in the yard at a reasonable rate. And yet, here we have Ramirez. When you see the filthy change you sort of get it: It tumbles startlingly out of the zone like a roller coaster's stomach-churning, accelerating descent—a Noé's Arc, if you will. Ramirez parlayed this successful pairing into a boatload of multi-inning turns, along with some spot-work as an opener. The limited arsenal will leave him open to some leaky outings, so more middle innings are likely what keeps him seaworthy in 2020.

YEAR	TEAM	LVL	AGE	WHIP	ERA	DRA	WARP	MPH	FB%	WHF	CSP
2017	PAW	AAA	27	1.15	3.51	3.51	1.0				
2017	LAA	MLB	27	0.84	2.16	3.65	0.1	91.7	25.9	14.7	42.4
2017	BOS	MLB	27	0.86	3.86	9.83	-0.2	91.9	50.7	16.9	48.8
2018	LAA	MLB	28	1.26	4.54	3.36	1.5	92.0	41.9	12.3	46.4
2019	LAA	MLB	29	1.17	3.99	3.87	1.1	91.0	28.4	14	47
2020	LAA	MLB	30	1.24	4.14	4.30	0.5	90.8	35	13.2	46

Noé Ramirez, continued

Pitch Shape vs LHH

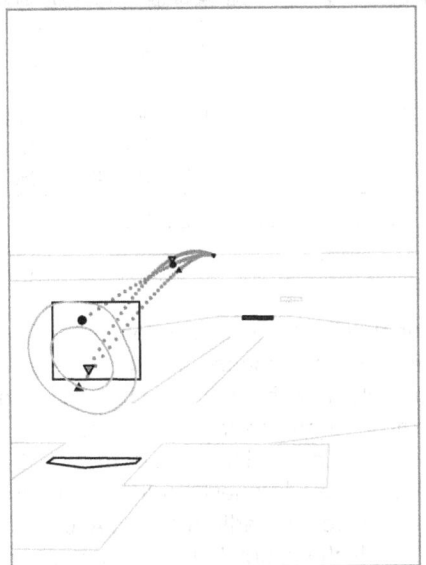

Pitch Shape vs RHH

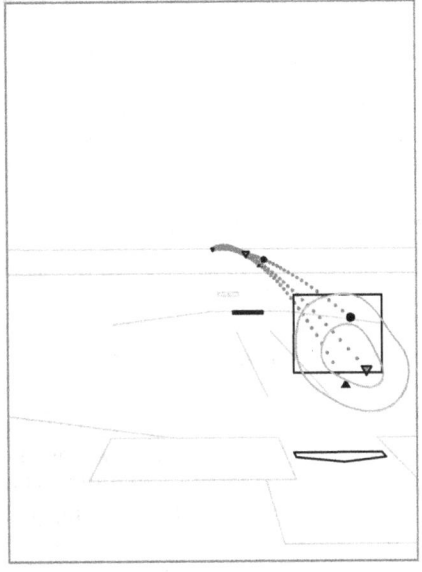

Type	Frequency	Velocity	H Movement	V Movement
● Fastball	28.4%	89.5 [92]	-6.8 [100]	-19.5 [91]
□ Sinker				
+ Cutter				
▲ Changeup	34.2%	84.5 [97]	-10.4 [103]	-38.3 [68]
× Splitter				
▽ Slider	37.4%	78 [73]	12.2 [130]	-43.2 [71]
◇ Curveball				
⬗ Slow Curveball				
✻ Knuckleball				
▼ Screwball				

Hansel Robles   RHP

Born: 08/13/90   Age: 29   Bats: R   Throws: R
Height: 6'0"   Weight: 220   Origin: International Free Agent, 2008

YEAR	TEAM	LVL	AGE	W	L	SV	G	GS	IP	H	HR	BB/9	K/9	K	GB%	BABIP
2017	LVG	AAA	26	0	1	4	18	0	23^1	27	5	5.4	8.5	22	36%	.319
2017	NYN	MLB	26	7	5	0	46	0	56^2	47	10	4.6	9.5	60	35%	.259
2018	LVG	AAA	27	0	0	2	8	0	7^2	7	1	5.9	8.2	7	61%	.273
2018	LAA	MLB	27	0	1	2	37	0	36^1	32	2	3.7	8.9	36	40%	.300
2018	NYN	MLB	27	2	2	0	16	0	19^2	21	7	4.6	10.5	23	28%	.298
2019	LAA	MLB	28	5	1	23	71	1	72^2	58	6	2.0	9.3	75	40%	.280
2020	LAA	MLB	29	3	3	34	63	0	67	61	9	3.4	10.0	75	38%	.297

Comparables: Arodys Vizcaíno, Bruce Rondón, Justin Grimm

If you're reading this comment, you're probably the type of fan who has pondered what walk-up or entrance music you would choose, should you ever have the opportunity. It's perhaps the most relatable thing that players do (even if we sometimes look down our collective noses at their questionable taste). Robles was one of us for many years, knowing his potential entrance music—the ominous, funereal theme of WWE's The Undertaker—but never getting quite to the closer's role, when he could blast his music from a stadium-sized PA to tens of thousands of fans. He spent a few years in Flushing, but Jeurys Familia would not yield. He waited. In 2018, he became part of a the Anaheim pen but couldn't get into the closing mix. Still he waited: dreaming, planning. By the time he took over for the deposed Cody Allen in May, Robles had an entire multimedia experience to accompany his entrance—the music, yes, but also a short film featuring a white horse, rose petals falling in slow motion through smoke, streaks of lightning. It lasts about two minutes and feels like outtakes from some obscure epic. It's a good thing Robles' production in the studio was matched by his production on the mound: The development of a dominant changeup helped him gallop away with the closer's job like the wild horse in his video. Now with some security in his role, we await the next development of the Hansel Robles Experience … Holograms? Flash mobs? Interpretive dance? May all our dreams be as fully realized as the moment in which Robles makes his way from the 'pen to the mound.

YEAR	TEAM	LVL	AGE	WHIP	ERA	DRA	WARP	MPH	FB%	WHF	CSP
2017	LVG	AAA	26	1.76	5.79	6.41	-0.3				
2017	NYN	MLB	26	1.34	4.92	5.63	-0.3	97.5	66.6	9.8	48
2018	LVG	AAA	27	1.57	3.52	4.86	0.0				
2018	LAA	MLB	27	1.29	2.97	4.90	0.0	99.0	67.5	12.5	49.5
2018	NYN	MLB	27	1.58	5.03	3.75	0.3	97.5	69.1	11.6	50.7
2019	LAA	MLB	28	1.02	2.48	3.67	1.3	99.3	56.3	13.5	49.8
2020	*LAA*	*MLB*	*29*	*1.29*	*3.92*	*4.05*	*0.8*	*98.0*	*62.3*	*12.3*	*49.4*

Los Angeles Angels 2020

Hansel Robles, continued

Pitch Shape vs LHH   **Pitch Shape vs RHH**

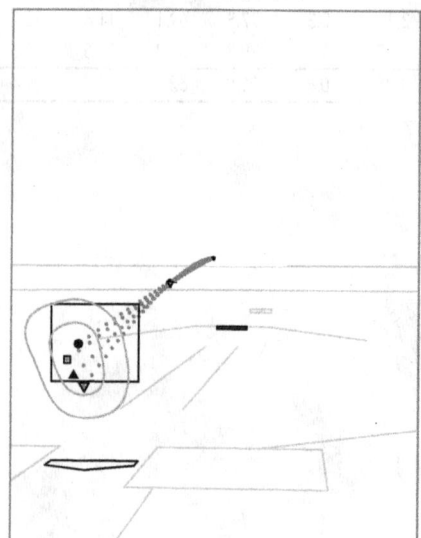 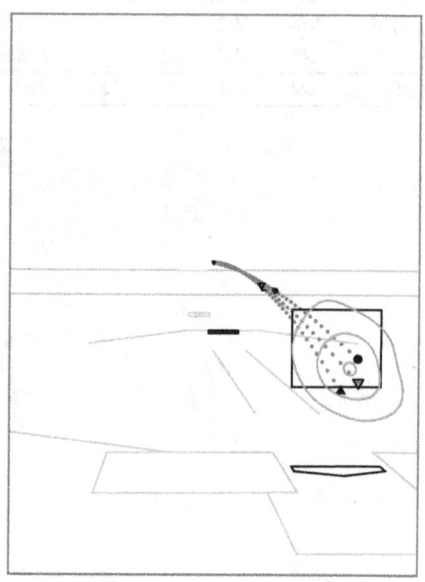

Type	Frequency	Velocity	H Movement	V Movement
● Fastball	53.3%	97.5 [114]	-11.2 [81]	-12 [110]
☐ Sinker				
+ Cutter				
▲ Changeup	23.0%	89.6 [116]	-11.7 [97]	-25.4 [106]
✕ Splitter				
▽ Slider	20.7%	89.7 [122]	0.8 [82]	-26.5 [119]
◇ Curveball				
✥ Slow Curveball				
✻ Knuckleball				
▼ Screwball				

Patrick Sandoval   LHP

Born: 10/18/96   Age: 23   Bats: L   Throws: L
Height: 6'3"   Weight: 190   Origin: Round 11, 2015 Draft (#319 overall)

YEAR	TEAM	LVL	AGE	W	L	SV	G	GS	IP	H	HR	BB/9	K/9	K	GB%	BABIP
2017	TCV	A-	20	1	1	0	4	4	19	19	0	2.8	13.3	28	47%	.404
2017	QUD	A	20	2	2	1	9	7	40	38	1	3.6	10.8	48	48%	.333
2018	QUD	A	21	7	1	1	14	10	65	58	4	1.5	9.8	71	48%	.305
2018	BCA	A+	21	2	0	1	5	3	23	12	1	1.6	10.2	26	46%	.216
2018	INL	A+	21	1	0	0	3	3	14^2	6	0	3.7	12.9	21	47%	.200
2018	MOB	AA	21	1	0	0	4	4	19^2	12	0	3.7	12.4	27	40%	.286
2019	MOB	AA	22	0	3	0	5	4	20	14	1	3.2	14.4	32	52%	.302
2019	SLC	AAA	22	4	4	0	15	15	60^1	84	7	5.2	9.8	66	47%	.401
2019	LAA	MLB	22	0	4	0	10	9	39^1	35	6	4.3	9.6	42	50%	.287
2020	LAA	MLB	23	6	4	0	36	13	83	70	11	4.2	9.9	91	46%	.282

Comparables: Hunter Wood, Jake Faria, Mitch Keller

Had everything gone according to plan, Sandoval would have likely remained in Salt Lake until September, and even then would have probably only been pressed into the odd relief or "opener" outing in Anaheim. Needless to say, the Angels needed him sooner, and as a starter. He managed to tread water in this role, with a tumbling curveball his strongest offering. Now with some major-league seasoning, Sandoval should get the chance to work on limiting walks and home runs, the main barrier for him (and most fringe-types) to overcome on the path to major-league value.

YEAR	TEAM	LVL	AGE	WHIP	ERA	DRA	WARP	MPH	FB%	WHF	CSP
2017	TCV	A-	20	1.32	3.79	3.86	0.3				
2017	QUD	A	20	1.35	3.83	4.65	0.3				
2018	QUD	A	21	1.06	2.49	3.25	1.4				
2018	BCA	A+	21	0.70	2.74	2.28	0.8				
2018	INL	A+	21	0.82	0.00	2.30	0.5				
2018	MOB	AA	21	1.02	1.37	2.89	0.6				
2019	MOB	AA	22	1.05	3.60	2.55	0.6				
2019	SLC	AAA	22	1.97	6.41	6.86	-0.1				
2019	LAA	MLB	22	1.37	5.03	4.35	0.6	94.8	46.5	14.3	45
2020	LAA	MLB	23	1.31	3.79	3.88	1.4	94.7	48.2	14.8	46.6

Los Angeles Angels 2020

Patrick Sandoval, continued

Pitch Shape vs LHH

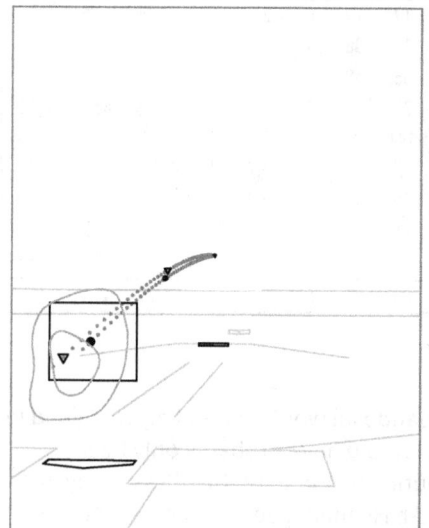

Pitch Shape vs RHH

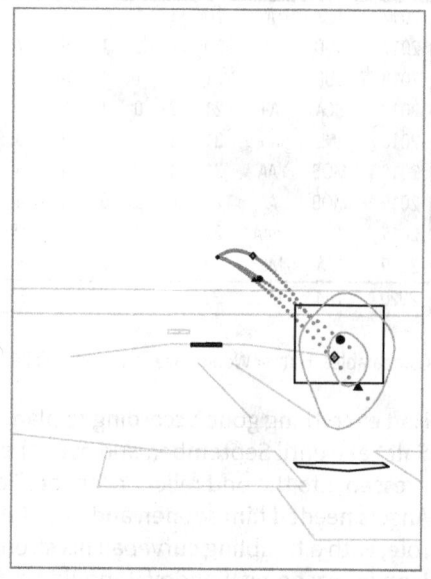

Type	Frequency	Velocity	H Movement	V Movement
● Fastball	46.5%	93 [102]	5.6 [106]	-13.9 [105]
☐ Sinker				
+ Cutter				
▲ Changeup	30.8%	83.6 [94]	10.8 [102]	-26.8 [102]
✕ Splitter				
▽ Slider	9.2%	86.5 [109]	-4.9 [100]	-29.6 [110]
◇ Curveball	13.4%	78 [98]	-3.6 [84]	-48 [99]
⊕ Slow Curveball				
✳ Knuckleball				
▼ Screwball				

Tyler Skaggs LHP

Born: 07/13/91　Age: 28　Bats: L　Throws: L
Height: 6'4"　Weight: 225　Origin: Round 1, 2009 Draft (#40 overall)

YEAR	TEAM	LVL	AGE	W	L	SV	G	GS	IP	H	HR	BB/9	K/9	K	GB%	BABIP
2017	SLC	AAA	25	0	1	0	3	3	10	14	0	5.4	6.3	7	54%	.400
2017	LAA	MLB	25	2	6	0	16	16	85	90	13	3.0	8.0	76	42%	.318
2018	LAA	MLB	26	8	10	0	24	24	125^1	127	14	2.9	9.3	129	45%	.328
2019	LAA	MLB	27	7	7	0	15	15	79^2	73	9	3.2	8.8	78	38%	.294
2020									No projection							

Skaggs died in a Southlake, Texas, hotel room in the early-morning hours of July 1, 2019, as his team was set to begin a four-game series with the Rangers. The coroner's report revealed that the Angels pitcher died of asphyxia while under the influence of fentanyl, oxycodone and alcohol. He was having an uneven but solid season as a starter, and had become a mainstay of the Angels rotation in his age-27 season. He and his wife, Carli, were married on New Year's Eve, 2018.

 It would be a small comfort if we could leave Skaggs' tragic death in the realm of the personal, here grieving the loss of ballplayer while those who knew him grieve the loss of a friend, teammate, husband, brother, son. But in October of last year, reporting by ESPN's T.J. Quinn revealed that Skaggs had been sold opioids by a team employee, Eric Kay, and that team officials were aware of Skaggs' use. Kay also stated that he had provided drugs to five other players while they were with the Angels. Kay claims he did not provide the opioids that contributed to Skaggs' death.

 In December, MLB introduced a new policy that includes opioid and cocaine testing, but most importantly, prioritizes treatment over punishment, only disciplining players who test positive after the violation of a prescribed treatment plan. One hopes this is a first step toward a drug testing and enforcement philosophy focused on empathy and care for those in need rather than punitive measures that scapegoat and criminalize individual users. Addressing this crisis on a systemic level, with intelligence and compassion, would be the best and most lasting tribute that could be paid to Skaggs.

YEAR	TEAM	LVL	AGE	WHIP	ERA	DRA	WARP	MPH	FB%	WHF	CSP
2017	SLC	AAA	25	2.00	8.10	7.48	-0.2				
2017	LAA	MLB	25	1.39	4.55	5.12	0.4	94.3	60.2	8.6	45.9
2018	LAA	MLB	26	1.33	4.02	3.86	2.1	94.3	58.6	12	48.9
2019	LAA	MLB	27	1.27	4.29	5.20	0.5	94.0	50.5	10	49
2020							No projection				

Tyler Skaggs, continued

Pitch Shape vs LHH

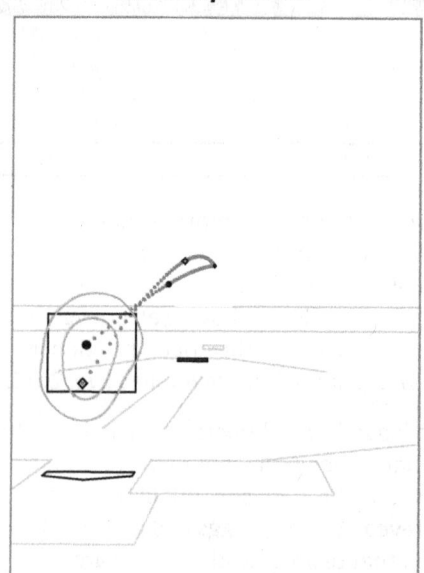

Pitch Shape vs RHH

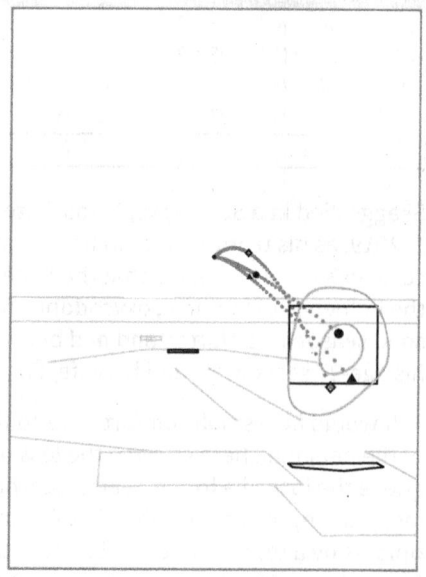

Type	Frequency	Velocity	H Movement	V Movement
● Fastball	50.5%	91.9 [99]	2 [122]	-14 [105]
☐ Sinker				
+ Cutter				
▲ Changeup	15.7%	84.4 [97]	9 [110]	-25.4 [106]
✕ Splitter				
▽ Slider				
◇ Curveball	33.8%	75.6 [90]	-8.7 [105]	-59.4 [75]
✤ Slow Curveball				
✱ Knuckleball				
▼ Screwball				

Jose Suarez LHP

Born: 01/03/98 Age: 22 Bats: L Throws: L
Height: 5'10" Weight: 225 Origin: International Free Agent, 2014

YEAR	TEAM	LVL	AGE	W	L	SV	G	GS	IP	H	HR	BB/9	K/9	K	GB%	BABIP
2017	ANG	RK	19	1	0	0	3	3	14	10	1	2.6	12.2	19	40%	.310
2017	BUR	A	19	5	1	0	12	12	54^2	49	7	3.0	11.7	71	48%	.333
2018	INL	A+	20	0	1	0	2	2	9	6	0	1.0	18.0	18	67%	.400
2018	MOB	AA	20	2	1	0	7	7	29^2	34	0	2.4	15.5	51	37%	.500
2018	SLC	AAA	20	1	4	0	17	17	78^1	81	5	4.0	8.4	73	48%	.336
2019	SLC	AAA	21	2	1	0	7	6	32^1	24	3	4.7	8.6	31	46%	.247
2019	LAA	MLB	21	2	6	0	19	15	81	100	23	3.7	8.0	72	38%	.325
2020	LAA	MLB	22	3	2	0	8	8	38	40	7	3.8	7.7	33	39%	.291

Comparables: Bryse Wilson, Jaime Barria, Lucas Giolito

Just because Suarez wasn't ready for prime time in 2019 doesn't mean he'll never be ready. Pressed into service in June, subsequent crises kept him in Anaheim for the bulk of the season. His four-seamer has some natural sink, which ran smack into plenty of uppercutting bats, frequently sending the balls into faraway, irretrievable places. Some more Triple-A time might be the best way forward for the 22-year-old in the hopes that the second run goes a little more smoothly than the messy debut.

YEAR	TEAM	LVL	AGE	WHIP	ERA	DRA	WARP	MPH	FB%	WHF	CSP
2017	ANG	RK	19	1.00	1.93	1.37	0.7				
2017	BUR	A	19	1.23	3.62	4.84	0.3				
2018	INL	A+	20	0.78	2.00	1.72	0.4				
2018	MOB	AA	20	1.42	3.03	4.91	0.1				
2018	SLC	AAA	20	1.48	4.48	4.26	1.1				
2019	SLC	AAA	21	1.27	3.62	2.58	1.3				
2019	LAA	MLB	21	1.64	7.11	8.98	-2.9	93.4	47.2	11.5	47.2
2020	LAA	MLB	22	1.46	5.40	5.31	0.1	93.4	49.2	11.9	49.2

Los Angeles Angels 2020

Jose Suarez, continued

Pitch Shape vs LHH

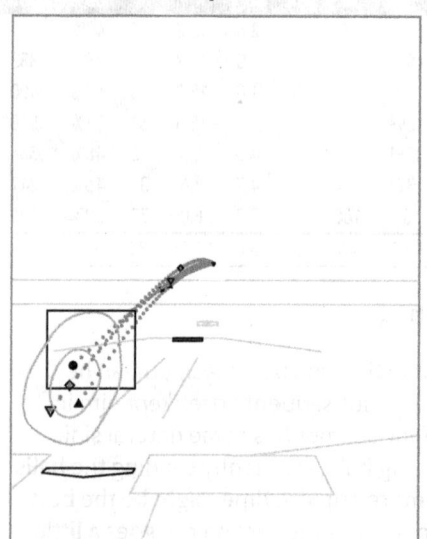

Pitch Shape vs RHH

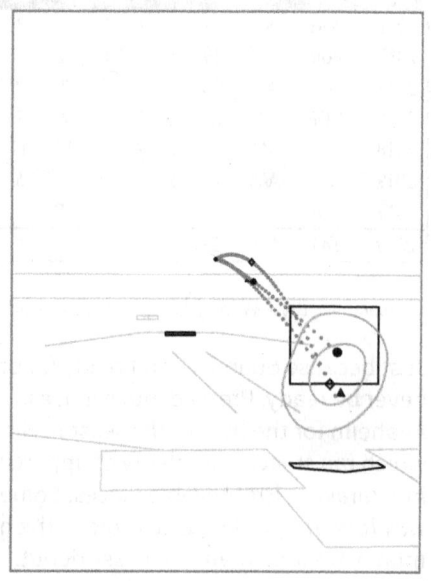

Type	Frequency	Velocity	H Movement	V Movement
● Fastball	46.9%	91.8 [98]	6.6 [101]	-15.4 [101]
☐ Sinker				
+ Cutter				
▲ Changeup	30.9%	81.9 [88]	7.5 [117]	-29.2 [95]
✕ Splitter				
▽ Slider	3.8%	81.1 [86]	-3.7 [95]	-37.8 [86]
◇ Curveball	18.1%	75.8 [91]	-10.4 [112]	-48.9 [97]
⊕ Slow Curveball				
✳ Knuckleball				
▼ Screwball				

Julio Teheran RHP

Born: 01/27/91   Age: 29   Bats: R   Throws: R
Height: 6'2"   Weight: 205   Origin: International Free Agent, 2007

YEAR	TEAM	LVL	AGE	W	L	SV	G	GS	IP	H	HR	BB/9	K/9	K	GB%	BABIP
2017	ATL	MLB	26	11	13	0	32	32	188^1	186	31	3.4	7.2	151	41%	.281
2018	ATL	MLB	27	9	9	0	31	31	175^2	122	26	4.3	8.3	162	40%	.217
2019	ATL	MLB	28	10	11	0	33	33	174^2	148	22	4.3	8.3	162	40%	.267
2020	LAA	MLB	29	10	8	0	28	28	140	127	25	3.8	8.4	131	39%	.269

Comparables: Ramon Martinez, Matt Cain, Michael Wacha

There aren't too many players in baseball who can be considered a crafty veteran by their age-28 season. Such was the case for Teheran entering the 2019 campaign, as his precipitous drop in velocity coincided with a similarly precipitous drop in prominence in Atlanta's rotation. Sure enough, he made one big adjustment to fight off Father Time's obscenely early attempt to reel him in. Teheran spent the 2019 season pitching exclusively from the stretch and it paid off—as the consistency allowed him to coerce more batters to meet him on his turf: just outside the strike zone. His velocity has continued to drop, which certainly played a role in Atlanta's decision to decline his 2020 option, but he's showing that young dogs can in fact learn some new tricks.

YEAR	TEAM	LVL	AGE	WHIP	ERA	DRA	WARP	MPH	FB%	WHF	CSP
2017	ATL	MLB	26	1.37	4.49	5.07	1.1	94.0	64.3	10	46.3
2018	ATL	MLB	27	1.17	3.94	4.06	2.5	92.7	61.9	12.3	44
2019	ATL	MLB	28	1.32	3.81	4.59	2.2	92.0	63.8	10.1	45.5
2020	LAA	MLB	29	1.33	4.42	4.52	1.6	92.1	63.3	10.8	45.2

Los Angeles Angels 2020

Julio Teheran, continued

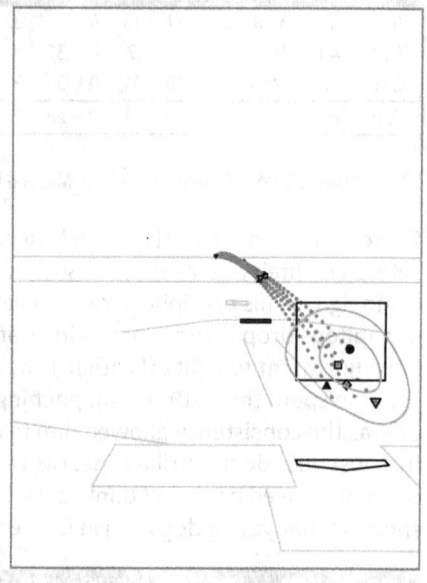

Pitch Shape vs LHH   **Pitch Shape vs RHH**

Type	Frequency	Velocity	H Movement	V Movement
● Fastball	41.5%	89.9 [93]	-5.5 [106]	-18.9 [92]
☐ Sinker	22.3%	89.4 [84]	-12.8 [99]	-26.2 [79]
+ Cutter				
▲ Changeup	8.7%	84 [96]	-13 [92]	-27.7 [99]
✕ Splitter				
▽ Slider	21.0%	82.3 [91]	3.2 [92]	-32.3 [102]
◇ Curveball	6.5%	74.8 [88]	10.9 [114]	-45.2 [105]
⊕ Slow Curveball				
✱ Knuckleball				
▼ Screwball				

PLAYER COMMENTS WITHOUT GRAPHS

Jordyn Adams OF
Born: 10/18/99 Age: 20 Bats: R Throws: R
Height: 6'2" Weight: 180 Origin: Round 1, 2018 Draft (#17 overall)

YEAR	TEAM	LVL	AGE	PA	R	2B	3B	HR	RBI	BB	K	SB	CS	AVG/OBP/SLG
2018	ANG	RK	18	82	8	2	2	0	5	10	23	5	2	.243/.354/.329
2018	ORM	RK	18	40	5	4	1	0	8	4	7	0	1	.314/.375/.486
2019	BUR	A	19	428	52	15	2	7	31	50	94	12	5	.250/.346/.358
2019	INL	A+	19	40	7	1	1	1	1	5	14	0	1	.229/.325/.400
2020	LAA	MLB	20	251	23	11	1	5	24	20	76	3	1	.226/.292/.342

Comparables: Trent Grisham, Joe Benson, Victor Robles

You could do worse for an organizational philosophy than "draft athletes and worry about the rest later." Adams joins a swelling cohort of Angels position-player prospects who have plenty of tools with varying degrees of refinement. What opened eyes about the former North Carolina football recruit was a strong performance in the notoriously hitter-hostile Midwest League, earning him a late-season call-up to the friendlier offensive climes of the Cal League, where he looks to start in the coming season. If the power isn't quite there yet, the patience and speed are, and Adams' development will be an above-the-fold story for Angels prospect watchers in 2020.

YEAR	TEAM	LVL	AGE	PA	DRC+	VORP	BABIP	BRR	FRAA	WARP
2018	ANG	RK	18	82	84	2.3	.362	0.9	CF(14): -4.2, RF(1): 0.0	-0.2
2018	ORM	RK	18	40	113	1.3	.379	-0.8	CF(8): 3.1	0.3
2019	BUR	A	19	428	123	20.6	.316	2.4	CF(73): -1.2, LF(9): 2.5	2.6
2019	INL	A+	19	40	94	2.0	.350	0.2	CF(4): 0.4, RF(2): -0.3	0.1
2020	LAA	MLB	20	251	71	-1.6	.317	-0.2	CF 0, LF 0	-0.1

Los Angeles Angels 2020

Jo Adell OF

Born: 04/08/99   Age: 21   Bats: R   Throws: R
Height: 6'3"   Weight: 215   Origin: Round 1, 2017 Draft (#10 overall)

YEAR	TEAM	LVL	AGE	PA	R	2B	3B	HR	RBI	BB	K	SB	CS	AVG/OBP/SLG
2017	ANG	RK	18	132	18	6	6	4	21	10	32	5	0	.288/.351/.542
2017	ORM	RK	18	90	25	5	2	1	9	4	17	3	2	.376/.411/.518
2018	BUR	A	19	108	23	7	1	6	29	11	26	4	1	.326/.398/.611
2018	INL	A+	19	262	46	19	3	12	42	15	63	9	2	.290/.345/.546
2018	MOB	AA	19	71	14	6	0	2	6	6	22	2	0	.238/.324/.429
2019	INL	A+	20	27	4	1	0	2	5	1	10	0	0	.280/.333/.560
2019	MOB	AA	20	182	28	15	0	8	23	19	41	6	0	.308/.390/.553
2019	SLC	AAA	20	132	22	11	0	0	8	10	43	1	0	.264/.321/.355
2020	LAA	MLB	21	245	26	15	1	8	29	19	78	3	1	.248/.313/.424

Comparables: Corey Seager, Ronald Acuña Jr., Austin Riley

According to the debut episode of BP's "Three-Quarters Delivery" podcast (cross-platform synergies, y'all!), Adell is an *icon*. Certainly, that's a weighty word for a dude who hasn't yet taken his first major-league licks. And if we're being honest, Adell's most recent minor-league stop, at Triple-A Salt Lake City, hints at some development yet to come for the 20-year-old (to be fair, he was never fully healthy after an early-season ankle/hammy injury). But one doesn't get "icon" from a stat line, however impressive. That title comes from qualitative, human observation—watching him calmly waggle his bat before uncorking a home-run swing, gracefully cover huge expanses of green as he tracks down a fly ball in center field, or conduct interviews and interact with fans with an easy charm and ready smile. In baseball terms, should the Angels and their fans be excited for Adell's arrival in 2020? Of course. But his iconic potential, particularly as a young black player in a sport with a dearth of African-American superstars, gives reason for those who simply root for baseball—its goodness, its relevance, its survival—to rejoice.

YEAR	TEAM	LVL	AGE	PA	DRC+	VORP	BABIP	BRR	FRAA	WARP
2017	ANG	RK	18	132	117	13.4	.361	1.9		0.5
2017	ORM	RK	18	90	133	7.3	.463	0.4		0.3
2018	BUR	A	19	108	164	12.4	.391	1.2	CF(16): -0.4, RF(3): -0.9	1.0
2018	INL	A+	19	262	142	21.9	.345	2.0	CF(36): -5.6, RF(8): -1.1	1.4
2018	MOB	AA	19	71	100	4.5	.333	-0.3	CF(17): -1.9	0.0
2019	INL	A+	20	27	115	3.0	.385	0.3	CF(3): 0.5, RF(2): -0.1	0.2
2019	MOB	AA	20	182	168	14.6	.369	0.5	RF(19): -1.2, CF(17): -3.5	1.5
2019	SLC	AAA	20	132	66	0.3	.410	2.5	RF(12): -0.5, LF(9): 0.6	0.0
2020	LAA	MLB	21	245	93	2.9	.345	0.0	RF -6	-0.3

Anthony Bemboom C

Born: 01/18/90 Age: 30 Bats: L Throws: R
Height: 6'2" Weight: 200 Origin: Round 22, 2012 Draft (#687 overall)

YEAR	TEAM	LVL	AGE	PA	R	2B	3B	HR	RBI	BB	K	SB	CS	AVG/OBP/SLG
2017	ABQ	AAA	27	160	20	8	2	4	20	24	30	0	0	.278/.390/.459
2018	ABQ	AAA	28	249	25	10	0	5	29	32	49	0	0	.232/.339/.351
2019	DUR	AAA	29	50	7	3	0	1	6	2	10	0	1	.213/.240/.340
2019	SLC	AAA	29	64	7	1	2	2	10	7	9	0	0	.316/.391/.509
2019	TBA	MLB	29	5	0	1	0	0	1	0	2	0	0	.400/.400/.600
2019	LAA	MLB	29	51	2	0	0	1	3	1	19	0	0	.102/.120/.163
2020	LAA	MLB	30	70	6	2	0	2	7	5	20	0	0	.201/.267/.321

Comparables: David Freitas, Mike Nickeas, Raffy Lopez

YEAR	TEAM	P. COUNT	FRM RUNS	BLK RUNS	THRW RUNS	TOT RUNS
2017	ABQ	5432	5.7	-0.4	0.2	5.3
2018	ABQ	7516	3.7	-0.1	0.3	3.7
2019	DUR	1141	2.6	0.0	0.0	2.6
2019	TBA	271	0.2	-1.1	0.3	-0.6
2019	LAA	2348	2.1	-0.1	0.0	2.0
2019	SLC	2161	0.0	0.0	0.2	0.2
2020	LAA	2717	1.9	-0.5	0.3	1.7

You struggle for eight years in three minor-league systems, you put in the work, you know you're not getting to the Show with your bat (you've never cracked double-digit homers or a .250 average outside the PCL), so you work with your pitchers, you work on your framing, your release—you just work. One day, you get to the show, and in your third game: it's the sixth inning, you've gone 2-for-2 with an RBI double, and what's more, you've piloted three pitchers through five shutout innings. You're most proud of that. Even the empty seats in Miami seem full of promise. Then, on a routine play, you tweak your knee and the brilliant night ends early. Your team? It signs a vet who goes on to an improbable comeback season. Good for him, you wish him nothing but the best. You? You get shipped to Anaheim, where you're the third catcher up, so: back to the minors, with some spot duty in September. There may not be many more extended stays in the show, but hey, you crossed the threshold. 2019 was a great year. You're a big-league catcher. Forever.

YEAR	TEAM	LVL	AGE	PA	DRC+	VORP	BABIP	BRR	FRAA	WARP
2017	ABQ	AAA	27	160	108	10.4	.330	-0.5	C(40): 6.7	1.6
2018	ABQ	AAA	28	249	81	4.0	.277	1.9	C(52): 7.4, 1B(1): 0.0	1.5
2019	DUR	AAA	29	50	62	-2.8	.243	0.3	C(8): 2.4	0.2
2019	SLC	AAA	29	64	95	4.0	.348	-0.4	C(15): 0.1	0.3
2019	TBA	MLB	29	5	79	0.2	.667	0.0	C(3): -0.6	0.0
2019	LAA	MLB	29	51	59	-0.1	.138	-0.2		0.2
2020	LAA	MLB	30	70	56	-0.9	.267	-0.1	C 2	0.1

Los Angeles Angels 2020

Trent Deveaux OF
Born: 05/04/00 Age: 20 Bats: R Throws: R
Height: 6'0" Weight: 160 Origin: International Free Agent, 2017

YEAR	TEAM	LVL	AGE	PA	R	2B	3B	HR	RBI	BB	K	SB	CS	AVG/OBP/SLG
2018	ANG	RK	18	194	20	5	0	1	11	24	68	7	4	.199/.309/.247
2019	ANG	RK	19	244	38	15	4	6	23	24	76	14	6	.247/.332/.437
2019	ORM	RK+	19	31	4	1	0	1	2	2	15	1	0	.172/.226/.310
2020	LAA	MLB	20	251	20	12	1	4	22	19	108	2	1	.192/.259/.306

Comparables: Brett Phillips, Aristides Aquino, Derrick Robinson

One can easily level the charge of "lazy comp" in pairing Deveaux with fellow 2017 signee D'Shawn Knowles, but, c'mon, it's practically unavoidable: both signed out of the Bahamas in the same year, both are speedy, athletic outfielders of similar size and build, both finished 2019 in the Pioneer League. It's difficult to say much more at this early point. Deveaux might have an edge in speed but Knowles has shown more power; Deveaux is older than Knowles but slightly below him on the organizational ladder. It's no sure thing that either player hits (in both literal and metaphorical senses), but 2020 will be a crucial year for this prospect's (oh please no...please don't do this) Deveaux-lopment.

YEAR	TEAM	LVL	AGE	PA	DRC+	VORP	BABIP	BRR	FRAA	WARP
2018	ANG	RK	18	194	67	-1.5	.327	1.4	CF(26): -6.1, RF(14): -0.3	-0.4
2019	ANG	RK	19	244	105	13.6	.351	0.3	CF(28): -5.0, LF(14): 0.1	0.4
2019	ORM	RK+	19	31	29	-1.7	.308	0.1		-0.1
2020	LAA	MLB	20	251	50	-8.2	.339	0.0	CF -2, RF 0	-1.1

Jeremiah Jackson SS

Born: 03/26/00 Age: 20 Bats: R Throws: R
Height: 6'0" Weight: 165 Origin: Round 2, 2018 Draft (#57 overall)

YEAR	TEAM	LVL	AGE	PA	R	2B	3B	HR	RBI	BB	K	SB	CS	AVG/OBP/SLG
2018	ANG	RK	18	91	13	4	2	5	14	7	25	6	1	.317/.374/.598
2018	ORM	RK	18	100	13	6	3	2	9	8	34	4	1	.198/.260/.396
2019	ORM	RK+	19	291	47	14	2	23	60	24	96	5	1	.266/.333/.605
2020	LAA	MLB	20	251	20	12	1	5	22	18	102	5	2	.181/.245/.304

Comparables: Carter Kieboom, Lewis Brinson, Clint Frazier

Like a number of the Angels' top prospects, Jackson is a toolsy, athletic, but still quite raw outfiel—wait, I'm sorry (holding finger to ear)—I'm being told that Jackson is a *shortstop*. A shortstop, in fact, who socked 23 bombs in a mere 291 plate appearances at short-season Orem. The good news and bad news both stem from the same source: he's only 19 and looks to fill out physically over the next few years. While a bigger body will likely move him off shortstop, it bodes very well for the continued development of his already-legit power bat. To be clear, the good news is much, much better than the bad.

YEAR	TEAM	LVL	AGE	PA	DRC+	VORP	BABIP	BRR	FRAA	WARP
2018	ANG	RK	18	91	147	13.9	.396	1.3	SS(21): -1.3	0.8
2018	ORM	RK	18	100	26	-1.4	.286	-0.3	SS(21): -1.7, 2B(1): 0.0	-0.7
2019	ORM	RK+	19	291	111	22.4	.315	1.0		1.3
2020	LAA	MLB	20	251	45	-9.6	.296	0.3	SS -1, 2B 0	-1.1

Jahmai Jones 2B

Born: 08/04/97   Age: 22   Bats: R   Throws: R
Height: 5'11"   Weight: 205   Origin: Round 2, 2015 Draft (#70 overall)

YEAR	TEAM	LVL	AGE	PA	R	2B	3B	HR	RBI	BB	K	SB	CS	AVG/OBP/SLG
2017	BUR	A	19	387	54	18	4	9	30	32	63	18	7	.272/.338/.425
2017	INL	A+	19	191	32	11	3	5	17	13	43	9	6	.302/.368/.488
2018	INL	A+	20	347	47	10	5	8	35	43	63	13	3	.235/.338/.383
2018	MOB	AA	20	212	33	10	4	2	20	24	51	11	1	.245/.335/.375
2019	MOB	AA	21	544	66	22	3	5	50	50	109	9	11	.234/.308/.324
2020	LAA	MLB	22	251	24	12	1	5	25	19	62	6	2	.228/.292/.362

Comparables: Victor Robles, Cole Tucker, Billy McKinney

For a few years, Jones was the pride of the Angels' farm system, but at some point reality outruns potential and you're a 22-year-old who just completed a first full year of Double-A with downturns in just about every aspect of your game. To be fair, Jones has learned a new position in the past couple of years, and well, maybe the upside was overplayed simply because there were no other prospects around to measure for scale. Now that the prospect fanfare has died down, the "post-hype sleeper" phase of his career is nicely teed up. Regardless of what the future holds, one never likes to see the hype train lose steam two stops before the big city.

YEAR	TEAM	LVL	AGE	PA	DRC+	VORP	BABIP	BRR	FRAA	WARP
2017	BUR	A	19	387	115	27.5	.309	5.7	CF(65): -3.4, LF(16): 0.5	2.1
2017	INL	A+	19	191	124	17.9	.379	2.0	CF(37): -9.7, LF(3): -0.5	0.2
2018	INL	A+	20	347	111	12.6	.272	1.5	2B(70): -6.9	0.8
2018	MOB	AA	20	212	104	5.7	.323	-1.5	2B(45): -1.7	0.4
2019	MOB	AA	21	544	79	2.8	.288	2.3	2B(108): 14.4, CF(7): 0.3	2.3
2020	LAA	MLB	22	251	73	-0.7	.289	0.0	2B 1, CF -2	-0.1

Ty Kelly 2B

Born: 07/20/88 Age: 31 Bats: B Throws: R
Height: 6'0" Weight: 180 Origin: Round 13, 2009 Draft (#386 overall)

YEAR	TEAM	LVL	AGE	PA	R	2B	3B	HR	RBI	BB	K	SB	CS	AVG/OBP/SLG
2017	NYN	MLB	28	1	0	0	0	0	0	0	1	0	0	.000/.000/.000
2017	PHI	MLB	28	104	11	7	0	2	14	8	24	0	0	.193/.260/.341
2018	LVG	AAA	29	424	60	24	5	8	52	48	92	2	1	.259/.348/.416
2018	NYN	MLB	29	12	1	0	0	0	0	1	2	0	0	.091/.167/.091
2019	SLC	AAA	30	317	37	12	3	1	22	32	80	3	2	.246/.325/.320
2020	LAA	MLB	31	251	22	11	1	3	21	25	66	1	1	.215/.298/.316

Comparables: Jemile Weeks, Mike Baxter, Earl Torgeson

Kelly announced his retirement in August 2019 after bouncing around between the Mets, Blue Jays, Phillies and Angels organizations. While he was never much more than a Quad-A bat, and perhaps barely that, he's showing some upside for a plus Twitter game in his post-baseball career. One such example: In his response to the Max Muncy-Madison Bumgarner kerfuffle, Kelly puts baseball beef in its proper perspective: "pimping home runs doesn't matter the planet is dying." Kelly may not be baseball's own Greta Thunberg, and he still has work to do to reach @BMcCarthy32 or @faridyu levels of tweet glory, but here's hoping that, in addition to his new role as third baseman for Team Israel, he finds time to keep tweeting about the larger contexts within which baseball—with its rituals, absurdities, and unwritten rules—is but a trivial pursuit.

YEAR	TEAM	LVL	AGE	PA	DRC+	VORP	BABIP	BRR	FRAA	WARP
2017	NYN	MLB	28	1	62	-0.3	--	0.0		0.0
2017	PHI	MLB	28	104	67	2.5	.231	0.9	2B(14): 0.3, LF(9): -1.0	0.2
2018	LVG	AAA	29	424	91	9.6	.326	-2.8	2B(45): -2.9, SS(42): -1.5	0.4
2018	NYN	MLB	29	12	82	-2.1	.111	0.1	2B(2): 0.0, 3B(1): 0.0	0.0
2019	SLC	AAA	30	317	52	-7.1	.337	-0.4	2B(67): -10.0, RF(9): -2.0	-1.9
2020	LAA	MLB	31	251	67	-3.0	.290	-0.3	2B -3, SS 0	-0.8

Los Angeles Angels 2020

D'Shawn Knowles OF
Born: 01/16/01   Age: 19   Bats: B   Throws: R
Height: 6'0"   Weight: 165   Origin: International Free Agent, 2017

YEAR	TEAM	LVL	AGE	PA	R	2B	3B	HR	RBI	BB	K	SB	CS	AVG/OBP/SLG
2018	ANG	RK	17	130	19	4	1	1	14	15	27	7	4	.301/.385/.381
2018	ORM	RK	17	123	27	9	2	4	15	13	38	2	3	.321/.398/.550
2019	ORM	RK+	18	290	38	11	4	6	28	26	76	5	4	.241/.310/.387
2020	LAA	MLB	19	251	22	11	1	4	22	24	89	3	2	.210/.291/.318

Comparables: Mike Trout, Anthony Santander, Juan Soto

Signed out of the Bahamas in 2017, Knowles did just fine in the Pioneer League in his age-18 season. Like fellow countryman and organizational mate Trent Deveaux, Knowles profiles as a speed-and-defense guy, but he also showed a soupçon of power in his rookie league stint, and room to further fill out portends a few more long balls in his future. Whether the Angels' organizational gambit of drafting and signing toolsy, speedy, athletic outfielders in bulk pays off, it certainly makes their lower-minors teams a lot more fun to watch.

YEAR	TEAM	LVL	AGE	PA	DRC+	VORP	BABIP	BRR	FRAA	WARP
2018	ANG	RK	17	130	132	9.6	.384	1.1	LF(13): -3.1, CF(9): -0.5	0.4
2018	ORM	RK	17	123	123	8.7	.463	0.3	CF(17): -1.2, RF(9): 1.8	0.4
2019	ORM	RK+	18	290	70	2.0	.307	-0.3		0.0
2020	LAA	MLB	19	251	66	-3.3	.328	-0.4	CF 0, RF 0	-0.4

Kevin Maitan 3B

Born: 02/12/00 Age: 20 Bats: B Throws: R
Height: 6'2" Weight: 190 Origin: International Free Agent, 2016

YEAR	TEAM	LVL	AGE	PA	R	2B	3B	HR	RBI	BB	K	SB	CS	AVG/OBP/SLG
2017	BRA	RK	17	37	5	3	0	0	3	2	10	1	0	.314/.351/.400
2017	DNV	RK	17	139	10	5	1	2	15	9	39	1	0	.220/.273/.323
2018	ORM	RK	18	284	42	13	1	8	26	19	66	1	2	.248/.306/.397
2019	BUR	A	19	532	56	11	3	12	46	39	164	7	4	.214/.278/.323
2020	LAA	MLB	20	251	21	10	1	5	23	17	90	0	0	.204/.262/.319

Comparables: Miguel Andújar, Alex Liddi, Renato Núñez

Literally the only way to put a positive spin on the trendline of Maitan is to remind yourself that, in 2019, he was a 19-year-old in the offense-smothering Midwest League. And, while he was bad, he wasn't, like, *historically* bad. There's not much else to recommend the two-time bonus baby: the wide-eyed Miggy comps, along with any chance at playing shortstop, have long since left the building. Stranger things have happened, and an age-20 season is by no means a late date to make a great leap forward, but Maitan will have to battle heroically against the forces of entropy to become a chapter, or even a paragraph, in an Angels success story rather than a mere footnote to Atlanta's failures.

YEAR	TEAM	LVL	AGE	PA	DRC+	VORP	BABIP	BRR	FRAA	WARP
2017	BRA	RK	17	37	101	2.1	.440	0.3	SS(5): -1.7	0.0
2017	DNV	RK	17	139	48	0.4	.295	-0.7	SS(30): 0.9	-0.2
2018	ORM	RK	18	284	64	7.5	.303	1.1	3B(40): 3.3, SS(21): -3.1	-0.4
2019	BUR	A	19	532	69	-5.5	.295	-1.9	3B(92): -6.9, 2B(21): -2.8	-1.4
2020	LAA	MLB	20	251	54	-7.4	.307	-0.3	3B -1, SS -1	-0.9

Los Angeles Angels 2020

Brandon Marsh OF

Born: 12/18/97 Age: 22 Bats: L Throws: R
Height: 6'4" Weight: 215 Origin: Round 2, 2016 Draft (#60 overall)

YEAR	TEAM	LVL	AGE	PA	R	2B	3B	HR	RBI	BB	K	SB	CS	AVG/OBP/SLG
2017	ORM	RK	19	192	47	13	5	4	44	9	35	10	2	.350/.396/.548
2018	BUR	A	20	154	26	12	1	3	24	21	40	4	0	.295/.390/.470
2018	INL	A+	20	426	59	15	6	7	46	52	118	10	4	.256/.348/.385
2019	MOB	AA	21	412	48	21	2	7	43	47	92	18	5	.300/.383/.428
2020	LAA	MLB	22	251	24	13	1	5	25	19	77	3	1	.246/.307/.375

Comparables: Tyler Austin, Jordan Schafer, Brett Jackson

We're not sure this is Billy Eppler's plan, but we need to be open to the possibility that the Angels GM has found the new market inefficiency in baseball: not enough football players—or at least players who could succeed at the other, lesser sport's skill positions. Along with the demonstrated gridiron success of D1-recruited high-school stars like Jordyn Adams and Michael Hermosillo, the Angels have the makings an up-and-coming backfield duo in the big-fast-strong combo of Jo Adell and the less-celebrated Marsh. With a frame that could bowl tacklers over at close range and speed that could lose them in the open field, Marsh has fortunately been able to translate his tools into the sport he actually plays. The full offensive package was on display in Double-A, which augurs well based on the tamer ball used at that level. Defensively, he'll probably end up in a corner, but has the tools to cover center if need be. Somewhat obscured by the luminous intensity of Adell's supernova, Marsh himself has enough light and energy to emerge as a minor star in his own constellation.

YEAR	TEAM	LVL	AGE	PA	DRC+	VORP	BABIP	BRR	FRAA	WARP
2017	ORM	RK	19	192	120	18.4	.417	3.2	RF(26): -1.9, CF(11): 1.5	0.7
2018	BUR	A	20	154	139	12.2	.400	2.9	CF(14): 1.2, RF(13): -1.3	1.4
2018	INL	A+	20	426	107	21.3	.356	4.3	CF(50): -0.8, RF(33): 3.0	2.2
2019	MOB	AA	21	412	141	27.8	.384	2.6	CF(54): -0.7, RF(19): 1.8	2.9
2020	LAA	MLB	22	251	81	2.1	.347	0.0	CF 0, RF 1	0.4

Shohei Ohtani RHP

Born: 07/05/94 Age: 25 Bats: L Throws: R
Height: 6'4" Weight: 210 Origin: International Free Agent, 2017

YEAR	TEAM	LVL	AGE	PA	R	2B	3B	HR	RBI	BB	K	SB	CS	AVG/OBP/SLG
2018	LAA	MLB	23	367	59	21	2	22	61	37	102	10	4	.285/.361/.564
2019	LAA	MLB	24	425	51	20	5	18	62	33	110	12	3	.286/.343/.505
2020	LAA	MLB	25	420	53	18	2	20	60	35	113	11	4	.261/.326/.477

Comparables: Dick Gernert, Gary Sánchez, Paul Goldschmidt

A mythical talent in a prosaic world, Ohtani is set to return to his full powers in 2020, once again bringing together what we only saw in fleeting glimpses during his 2018 debut: a pitcher virtually unhittable when he can command his high-90s cheese alongside his devastating splitter and slider, and ... and ... an offensive force with silly power to all fields and blazing speed to boot. There's a small sadness in the fact that, in a different age, Ohtani would have no such restrictions on the display of his talents: he could pitch every fifth day as long as he wants, roam the outfield on his off days, hit in the middle of the order every day, and have full rein to run wild on the bases. To imagine this alternate reality is to approach the Platonic ideal of a baseball player. In the real, imperfect world, we'll have to settle for the actual Ohtani, who still has a chance, even in a part-time, designated-hitting offensive role, to be a historically unique and generationally valuable talent. Lucky us.

YEAR	TEAM	LVL	AGE	PA	DRC+	VORP	BABIP	BRR	FRAA	WARP
2018	LAA	MLB	23	367	129	22.8	.350	-2.3		1.7
2019	LAA	MLB	24	425	106	10.0	.354	-1.5		0.8
2020	LAA	MLB	25	420	110	19.0	.320	0.0		2.0

Jared Walsh 1B

Born: 07/30/93 Age: 26 Bats: L Throws: L
Height: 6'0" Weight: 210 Origin: Round 39, 2015 Draft (#1185 overall)

YEAR	TEAM	LVL	AGE	PA	R	2B	3B	HR	RBI	BB	K	SB	CS	AVG/OBP/SLG
2017	INL	A+	23	306	43	29	1	8	52	26	72	1	0	.331/.395/.531
2017	MOB	AA	23	74	7	3	0	3	9	3	29	1	0	.232/.274/.406
2018	INL	A+	24	178	28	8	1	13	36	24	50	0	1	.275/.365/.604
2018	MOB	AA	24	173	26	13	0	8	26	21	48	1	0	.289/.382/.537
2018	SLC	AAA	24	198	32	13	0	8	37	16	56	0	0	.270/.333/.478
2019	SLC	AAA	25	454	90	30	0	36	86	59	115	0	0	.325/.423/.686
2019	LAA	MLB	25	87	6	5	1	1	5	6	35	0	0	.203/.276/.329
2020	LAA	MLB	26	35	4	1	0	2	5	3	11	0	0	.237/.310/.454

Comparables: Harry Agganis, Trey Mancini, Dale Long

Somewhere between the full-on two-way excellence of Shohei Ohtani and the wacky novelty of position players like, say, Stevie Wilkerson notching saves with 56 mph junk (against the Angels, no less!) exists a grayer area occupied by folks like Walsh. For all intents and purposes, he's an interesting corner-infield bat whose improved patience was overshadowed by out-of-nowhere, PCL-silly power numbers in 2019. Along the way the Angels have nurtured his pitching dreams, which are not completely crazy given his low-90s fastball and competent secondaries. At least there's some credible hope that he can serve a major-league roster in a mop-up role. None of this is to say that Walsh has much of a ceiling on either side of the ledger, and the cynical among us might foresee an increase in Walshes—players just good enough to fill out the ends of both benches—as teams bow to the gods Efficiency and Optimization. If Ohtani is the generational pitcher-hitter unicorn, then Walsh might be the workhorse, heralding a more realistic trend toward the two*ish*-way player.

YEAR	TEAM	LVL	AGE	PA	DRC+	VORP	BABIP	BRR	FRAA	WARP
2017	INL	A+	23	306	157	20.5	.423	-1.9	1B(51): 1.5, RF(12): -1.7	2.0
2017	MOB	AA	23	74	76	-0.5	.351	-0.7	1B(18): -1.1, RF(1): -0.1	-0.3
2018	INL	A+	24	178	166	15.3	.308	-0.6	1B(26): 0.3, RF(5): 0.7	1.4
2018	MOB	AA	24	173	132	9.6	.372	-0.8	1B(37): 2.0, P(2): 0.0	0.9
2018	SLC	AAA	24	198	114	7.1	.345	1.8	RF(27): -5.7, LF(14): -1.7	0.2
2019	SLC	AAA	25	454	145	45.4	.374	0.7	1B(58): 4.6, P(12): 0.5	3.6
2019	LAA	MLB	25	87	59	-3.3	.349	-0.2		-0.3
2020	LAA	MLB	26	35	97	0.4	.308	-0.1	1B 0	0.1

Keynan Middleton RHP

Born: 09/12/93 Age: 26 Bats: R Throws: R
Height: 6'3" Weight: 215 Origin: Round 3, 2013 Draft (#95 overall)

YEAR	TEAM	LVL	AGE	W	L	SV	G	GS	IP	H	HR	BB/9	K/9	K	GB%	BABIP
2017	SLC	AAA	23	0	0	2	10	0	12^2	11	0	2.8	5.7	8	36%	.282
2017	LAA	MLB	23	6	1	3	64	0	58^1	60	11	2.8	9.7	63	38%	.318
2018	LAA	MLB	24	0	0	6	16	0	17^2	14	1	4.6	8.2	16	33%	.295
2019	LAA	MLB	25	0	0	0	11	0	7^2	4	0	8.2	7.0	6	35%	.200
2020	LAA	MLB	26	2	2	2	46	0	49	42	8	4.3	10.0	54	36%	.277

Comparables: Joe Musgrove, Chase Whitley, Dovydas Neverauskas

For a few weeks early in the 2018 season, Middleton had been bestowed with the mantle that all relief pitchers covet: The Closer. He'd earned that role through a strong 2017, an ability to get out lefties as well as righties, and a bullpen that was bereft of other options. Oh, he also got it by throwing major heat, which may or may not have been a proximate cause of a UCL tear. Middleton's September comeback was enough to feel good about, but not conclusive enough to know where he stands coming into 2020. Should the heat return to full boil, Middleton may again enter the end-game conversation. If not, the innings may come in a more nominatively appropriate way: in the middle, and by the ton.

YEAR	TEAM	LVL	AGE	WHIP	ERA	DRA	WARP	MPH	FB%	WHF	CSP
2017	SLC	AAA	23	1.18	2.84	3.44	0.3				
2017	LAA	MLB	23	1.34	3.86	3.80	0.9	99.4	62.6	18.2	48.7
2018	LAA	MLB	24	1.30	2.04	5.55	-0.1	98.8	64.4	11	44.7
2019	LAA	MLB	25	1.43	1.17	5.25	0.0	96.5	57.3	10.5	43.5
2020	LAA	MLB	26	1.34	4.26	4.37	0.4	98.5	63.4	15.5	46

Shohei Ohtani   RHP

Born: 07/05/94   Age: 25   Bats: L   Throws: R
Height: 6'4"   Weight: 210   Origin: International Free Agent, 2017

YEAR	TEAM	LVL	AGE	W	L	SV	G	GS	IP	H	HR	BB/9	K/9	K	GB%	BABIP
2018	LAA	MLB	23	4	2	0	10	10	51^2	38	6	3.8	11.0	63	40%	.269
2020	LAA	MLB	25	8	6	0	21	21	116	98	19	4.3	12.3	158	41%	.303

Comparables: Matt Harvey, Chris Archer, Zac Gallen

A mythical talent in a prosaic world, Ohtani is set to return to his full powers in 2020, once again bringing together what we only saw in fleeting glimpses during his 2018 debut: a pitcher virtually unhittable when he can command his high-90s cheese alongside his devastating splitter and slider, and ... *and* ... an offensive force with silly power to all fields and blazing speed to boot. There's a small sadness in the fact that, in a different age, Ohtani would have no such restrictions on the display of his talents: he could pitch every fifth day as long as he wants, roam the outfield on his off days, hit in the middle of the order every day, and have full rein to run wild on the bases. To imagine this alternate reality is to approach the Platonic ideal of a baseball player. In the real, imperfect world, we'll have to settle for the actual Ohtani, who still has a chance, even in a part-time, designated-hitting offensive role, to be a historically unique and generationally valuable talent. Lucky us.

YEAR	TEAM	LVL	AGE	WHIP	ERA	DRA	WARP	MPH	FB%	WHF	CSP
2018	LAA	MLB	23	1.16	3.31	3.46	1.1	100.3	46.4	15.5	47.6
2020	LAA	MLB	25	1.32	4.13	4.22	1.7	100.0	47.5	15.8	48.8

LINEOUTS

Hitters

HITTER	POS	TEAM	LVL	AGE	PA	R	2B	3B	HR	RBI	BB	K	SB	CS	AVG/OBP/SLG	DRC+	WARP
Kaleb Cowart	INF	MOB	AA	27	42	4	1	0	1	2	2	11	0	0	.179/.214/.282	50	0.0
	INF	SLC	AAA	27	317	42	15	4	8	60	25	55	3	4	.289/.345/.453	86	0.4
	INF	LAA	MLB	27	26	1	3	0	0	1	1	7	1	0	.160/.192/.280	76	0.0
Orlando Martinez	OF	INL	A+	21	422	55	21	4	12	49	36	79	5	4	.263/.325/.434	111	1.9
Adrian Rondon	3B	ORM	Rk+	20	122	19	7	2	5	19	10	21	2	0	.315/.369/.550	132	0.6
	3B	BUR	A	20	168	10	4	0	0	8	8	45	3	3	.231/.280/.256	70	-0.5
Livan Soto	SS	ANG	Rk	19	29	4	2	0	0	1	1	4	0	2	.214/.241/.286	87	0.1
	SS	BUR	A	19	282	24	5	0	1	20	32	40	6	2	.220/.311/.253	82	-0.1
Wilfredo Tovar	SS	SLC	AAA	27	349	53	17	6	4	57	19	45	3	6	.321/.355/.446	81	0.1
	SS	LAA	MLB	27	88	5	5	0	0	5	5	15	0	0	.193/.239/.253	64	0.2
Taylor Ward	3B	SLC	AAA	25	512	102	34	1	27	71	80	101	11	5	.306/.427/.584	139	4.6
	3B	LAA	MLB	25	48	4	3	0	1	2	6	23	0	0	.190/.292/.333	60	-0.2

"Utility" is often used in a quietly pejorative way: the player so designated is not good but can at least be average in diverse ways and at multiple positions. **Kaleb Cowart** dipped below that standard in 2019, revealing the precise moment at which "utility" adds an "f" as its first letter. ⓥ **Orlando Martinez**, a 22-year-old 2017 signee out of Cuba is, in keeping with organizational type, a toolsy, athletic outfielder. Unlike some of his organizational counterparts, he has good shot to be useful in a fourth-outfielder role sooner, rather than later thanks to an advanced approach. ⓥ A second-round pick who chose the dream of playing in Anaheim over the certainty of college ball in Berkeley, **Kyren Paris** has a first name that shares two of three syllables with a recent Star Wars villain. With his slick glove and slight frame, it remains to be seen if the force can awaken his bat. ⓥ Acquired from the Rays for cash, former high-profile J2 signee **Adrian Rondon** has been on a similarly disappointing path as new org-mate Kevin Maitan. Rondon did what he was supposed to do as a 20-year-old in rookie ball, but was flummoxed after a mid-season promotion to Low-A. Without significant growth in the bat, Rondon will be a lot closer to being Ron-done. ⓥ The fact that feather-hitting shortstop **Livan Soto** may have passed the more celebrated prospect-also-stripped-from-Atlanta, Kevin Maitan, will mean very little to future baseball historians when both players top out at Double-A in 2022. ⓥ A shortstop who, before last June, had most recently appeared in the majors in 2014, **Wilfredo Tovar**—somehow—parlayed five subpar hitting seasons in Triple-A into a mid-season call-up to Anaheim. This speaks well of Tovar's persistence, but less well of the Angels organizational depth. ⓥ After two cups of coffee that were more Yuban than Yirgacheffe, it's easy to dismiss **Taylor Ward** as a Quad-

Los Angeles Angels 2020

A superstar. Yet, that advanced plate approach calls us back to the urn again, hoping that, when we weren't looking, someone brewed up a fresh pot of the good stuff.

Pitchers

PITCHER	TEAM	LVL	AGE	W	L	SV	G	GS	IP	H	HR	BB/9	K/9	K	GB%	WHIP	ERA	DRA	WARP
Stiward Aquino	ANG	Rk	20	0	4	0	8	8	21	27	1	4.3	11.1	26	39%	1.76	7.71	7.50	-0.3
	ORM	Rk+	20	0	1	0	4	4	15²	19	3	3.4	13.2	23	43%	1.60	5.74	5.50	0.1
Kyle Bradish	INL	A+	22	6	7	0	24	18	101	90	9	4.7	10.7	120	45%	1.42	4.28	4.85	0.1
Jesus Castillo	MOB	AA	23	6	6	2	38	12	99²	100	4	2.3	7.2	80	51%	1.26	2.71	4.80	0.0
William English	ANG	Rk	18	0	2	0	7	6	17¹	15	2	8.3	13.0	25	38%	1.79	5.71	5.89	0.0
	ORM	Rk+	18	0	0	0	2	2	7	4	2	5.1	16.7	13	33%	1.14	3.86	5.53	0.1
Aaron Hernandez	INL	A+	22	1	4	0	20	15	72²	75	6	5.7	10.0	81	40%	1.67	4.46	6.07	-1.0
Jake Jewell	SLC	AAA	26	4	4	8	34	0	37²	42	3	4.1	9.8	41	50%	1.57	5.26	4.12	0.8
	LAA	MLB	26	0	0	0	18	0	26¹	28	8	2.7	7.9	23	62%	1.37	6.84	4.89	0.1
Kyle Keller	NWO	AAA	26	2	3	10	37	0	54	44	8	3.5	12.2	73	35%	1.20	4.50	3.14	1.6
	MIA	MLB	26	0	0	0	10	0	10²	5	3	6.8	9.3	11	24%	1.22	3.38	5.88	-0.1
Luis Madero	INL	A+	22	1	0	0	4	3	16	15	0	3.9	12.9	23	40%	1.38	1.12	4.98	0.0
	MOB	AA	22	5	11	0	20	19	89²	117	11	2.4	7.5	75	49%	1.57	5.72	6.41	-1.6
Parker Markel	ARK	AA	28	2	0	1	5	0	7²	2	0	2.3	21.1	18	29%	0.52	0.00	1.42	0.3
	IND	AAA	28	1	0	0	4	0	6	0	0	4.5	19.5	13	100%	0.50	0.00	1.16	0.3
	TAC	AAA	28	2	0	8	22	0	27²	13	3	6.8	14.3	44	44%	1.23	2.60	1.71	1.2
	SEA	MLB	28	0	0	0	5	0	4²	10	3	7.7	5.8	3	25%	3.00	15.43	9.53	-0.2
	PIT	MLB	28	0	1	0	15	0	17¹	16	3	6.8	10.9	21	41%	1.67	5.71	5.42	0.0
Isaac Mattson	INL	A+	23	3	0	0	8	0	20¹	8	1	4.0	13.3	30	46%	0.84	0.89	2.15	0.6
	MOB	AA	23	3	3	0	24	0	43²	30	3	2.7	12.6	61	52%	0.98	2.68	3.04	0.8
	SLC	AAA	23	0	0	1	5	0	9¹	9	0	4.8	18.3	19	39%	1.50	3.86	1.62	0.4
Mike Mayers	MEM	AAA	27	0	1	6	20	1	20	21	4	3.2	10.8	24	55%	1.40	3.15	4.23	0.4
	SLN	MLB	27	0	1	0	16	0	19	21	3	5.2	7.6	16	22%	1.68	6.63	8.02	-0.5
JC Ramirez	INL	A+	30	0	1	0	4	2	7	8	3	2.6	9.0	7	43%	1.43	6.43	4.25	0.1
	SLC	AAA	30	1	2	0	12	8	41	49	7	4.0	5.7	26	43%	1.63	6.59	5.48	0.5
	LAA	MLB	30	0	0	0	5	0	8	8	1	1.1	4.5	4	50%	1.12	4.50	5.26	0.0
Neil Ramirez	COH	AAA	30	2	1	2	25	0	29¹	28	7	3.4	13.8	45	28%	1.33	4.91	3.60	0.7
	CLE	MLB	30	0	1	0	16	0	16²	18	5	4.9	9.7	18	25%	1.62	5.40	7.97	-0.5
	TOR	MLB	30	0	0	0	6	1	8¹	8	2	6.5	6.5	6	20%	1.68	5.40	8.66	-0.3
Chris Rodriguez	INL	A+	20	0	0	0	3	3	9¹	6	0	3.9	12.5	13	68%	1.07	0.00	3.14	0.2
Jose Rodriguez	MOB	AA	23	0	2	0	5	5	17¹	24	2	3.1	12.5	24	51%	1.73	7.27	5.16	0.0
	SLC	AAA	23	3	3	2	18	2	44¹	48	7	4.5	9.1	45	41%	1.58	6.29	4.57	0.7
	LAA	MLB	23	0	1	0	9	1	19²	17	5	5.0	5.9	13	40%	1.42	2.75	6.62	-0.3
Jose Soriano	BUR	A	20	5	6	0	17	15	77²	53	5	5.6	9.7	84	55%	1.30	2.55	4.40	0.7
Hector Yan	BUR	A	20	4	5	1	26	20	109	74	5	4.3	12.2	148	41%	1.16	3.39	3.76	1.7

Described by one of BP's prospect analysts as "goofy-long," **Stiward Aquino** came back from TJ surgery with a few more ticks on his fastball. 2020 will be

Angels Player Analysis - 103

the year to watch for command and refinement, and if both arrive, Stiward will be headed skyward. ⓘ Maybe it was growing up in the thin, desert air of the Phoenix area, and going to college in similar climes at New Mexico State, but **Kyle Bradish** handled the pitcher's nightmare of the Cal League respectably well in his first season of pro ball. He's likely a relief arm, but one that could move quickly. ⓘ In his second full year at Double-A, former Cubs prospect **Jesus Castillo** began to fulfill the prophecy: he shall be a reliever, and he shall induce ground balls, but it will be a small miracle if he saves. ⓘ Formerly William English, now **William Holmes**, the two-way player from Detroit lost most of 2019 to injury, and 2020 will see him try to pump up the volume on both tracks of his stereophonic game. ⓘ 2018 third-round draftee **Aaron Hernandez** held serve in his first pro season, impressing with strikeouts and disappointing with spotty command. 2020 could be the fork in the road for his future role, and he's likely to take a relief path. ⓘ Unless he can develop more facets to his game, **Jake Jewell** can hope to shine only in low-leverage relief settings. Otherwise, it all looks pretty dull for the 26-year-old. ⓘ **Kyle Keller** pitched his way into the Marlins bullpen by the end of 2019 by striking out more than 12 batters per nine with the Baby Cakes; however, he struggled to find the zone in any consistent manner during his cup of coffee in Miami and bullpen slots are getting harder to come by with increasing organizational depth. ⓘ **Luis Madero** does a good job of throwing strikes, but he's going to need to stop allowing so many hits if he wants to make his big-league debut in 2020. ⓘ Late-bloomer **Parker Markel** and his mid-90s gas went from the American Association in 2018 to an array of teams plucking him from waivers in 2019. Hopping from org to org sure beats the alternative. ⓘ Though great things were not expected from college righty **Isaac Mattson**, he had himself a great year, with two promotions, a dominant stint in the Arizona Fall League, and a strikeout rate that makes you think there's more upside than his passable three-pitch mix actually holds. ⓘ **Mike Mayers** lost nearly two miles per hour off his fastball from 2018 to 2019, reducing his outings from pleasant enough to a horror show. His name is pronounced "Myers" and he passed through waivers before later being re-added to the 40-man roster—meaning he reappears just when you think he's history. If he ends up in Peoria we'll begin to wonder if Dr. Loomis is required. ⓘ As recently as 2017, **JC Ramírez** was an unlikely rotation piece for the Angels. Since then, it's all gone to pieces: working back from UCL surgery, Ramirez only logged 14 2/3 major-league innings over the last two years—not enough for the Angels to keep him around for 2020. ⓘ After what looked like a much-delayed breakout in 2018, **Neil Ramírez** found himself with a ground-ball rate in the low 20s and a lot more spare time on his hands in September. ⓘ Dogged by a back injury that has allowed him to pitch only nine innings over the past two seasons, **Chris Rodriguez** is a righty with a major-league arsenal, which is why the Angels will practice all the patience necessary to get him back on the mound—hopefully for a full 2020. ⓘ If you *only* let opponents score on home runs, maybe you can get away with allowing more than two per nine, or barely striking out more than you walk - or both. Somehow, it seems unlikely the **Jose Rodriguez** Method will catch on. ⓫ The big body and raw stuff alone could power **Jose Soriano**'s path to major-league relevance. Developing a consistent repeatable motion will be key in making that relevance happen sooner and in a starter's role. ⓫ Who can strike out north of 12 hitters per nine while firing mid-90s with movement from the left side? Why, **Hector Yan** can. His smaller frame points toward a relief role, which could jump the 20-year-old up the ladder quickly.

Angels Prospects

The State of the System
Still significantly improved compared to a couple years ago, but beyond the icon up top it remains a fairly shallow system reliant on untapped upside at the lower levels eventually bearing fruit.

The Top Ten

─────── ★ ★ ★ *2020 Top 101 Prospect* **#2** ★ ★ ★ ───────

1 **Jo Adell OF** OFP: 70 ETA: 2020
Born: 04/08/99 Age: 21 Bats: R Throws: R Height: 6'3" Weight: 215
Origin: Round 1, 2017 Draft (#10 overall)

The Report: There aren't many pages of Adell's prospect story left to read that aren't already slathered in drool, and he will enter the 2020 season perched again—for a final time—among the best couple prospects in the entire world. That he is even still eligible for this list resulted not from a lack of level-appropriate offensive prowess, but from lost developmental time after a gruesome leg injury in the spring and the negative subsequent effects that shelving allegedly had on his ability to track fly balls in a corner spot. This is a true five-tool talent, however, and those types don't wallow well or for long against Triple-A competition. He'll flank Mike Trout in Anaheim rather than supplant him in center, but the glove and speed for a theoretical up-the-middle assignment remain. The bat is now seasoned and cooked to perfection, and he'll have as much of a chance as any rookie to hit the ground hitting against the best pitchers in the game. On-base skills, power, and value-added baserunning and defense is some kind of package.

Variance: Low, at least insofar as any young player's risk factor can be discounted. Loads of talent and plenty of track record make him one of the "safer" high-end prospects around, and it would be quite a shock to the system if a healthy Adell does not go on to at least a first-division career.

Ben Carsley's Fantasy Take: *[Extremely James Blake voice]: You're beautiful. You're beautiful. You're beautiful, it's true.*

Wander Franco is a perfectly reasonable choice, but for my money, Adell is the top dynasty prospect in baseball. .300/30/100 with 20-plus steals will be within his reach some day. Treasure him.

Los Angeles Angels 2020

───── ★ ★ ★ *2020 Top 101 Prospect* **#51** ★ ★ ★ ─────

2 **Brandon Marsh   OF**   OFP: 60   ETA: Late 2020
Born: 12/18/97   Age: 22   Bats: L   Throws: R   Height: 6'4"   Weight: 215
Origin: Round 2, 2016 Draft (#60 overall)

The Report: Selected in the second round in 2016, Marsh is an intimidating and agile athlete, standing 6-foot-4 with an extra-large frame. He missed a bunch of Double-A seasoning in 2019 due to a leg injury, but showed off his improving hit tool when healthy. His bat-to-ball skills make him a true gap-to-gap hitter, and plenty of strength lets him drive the ball with some sizzle. Once he finds a gap, his plus wheels are a sight to see. He moves very well for his size, and should remain a threat to swipe a few bags through maturity. His power tool is tracking to play about average, but there is plenty of muscle and strength that points to some potential for swing-change-induced growth with launch angle adjustments. Patrolling the outfield, Marsh can play all three spots, with plus potential in the corners. There's enough to profile as a true center fielder, but as with Adell it might not be enough to supplant Trout, and he will likely slide to right in Anaheim. That challenge will not be a problem, as he has a plus arm to keep runners at bay. Marsh has an intriguing tool set that retains some room for growth and projection. He could very well find himself in an outfield next to Trout and Adell one day.

Variance: High. As mentioned, his ability to make hard contact has been impressive of late. But with just average power, Marsh will need to max out his hit tool to be a consistent threat offensively.

Ben Carsley's Fantasy Take: For how toolsy he is and how close he is to the majors, I'm not sure why Marsh doesn't get more love in fantasy circles. Even if the power never fully materializes and he's only a 15-homer guy, Marsh has the bat and legs to serve as a well-rounded OF4. If he is able to leverage his big boy frame into more pop, we could be looking at a high-end OF3 instead. Given that he should challenge for MLB plate appearances late this year or early next, that makes Marsh a borderline top-50 dynasty prospect for me. I'm a fan, even if part of me still worries the Angels will block him by re-signing Kole Calhoun to a 12-year extension.

───── ★ ★ ★ *2020 Top 101 Prospect* **#72** ★ ★ ★ ─────

3 **Jordyn Adams   OF**   OFP: 60   ETA: 2021
Born: 10/18/99   Age: 20   Bats: R   Throws: R   Height: 6'2"   Weight: 180
Origin: Round 1, 2018 Draft (#17 overall)

The Report: The Angels' 2018 first-round pick passed on a UNC football scholarship for professional baseball and his first full pro season went well, ending with a cup of coffee at High-A Inland Empire. Adams utilizes his exceptional athleticism to roam the outfield with plus-range, while also showing an above-average throwing arm and the direct routes and nose for the ball that you'd expect from a heavily-recruited wide receiver. His 70-grade speed is progressively adapting to the basepaths, as he found success on 16-of-22 stolen base attempts last season. Adams has shown an advanced process and approach at the plate, evidenced in his career .353 OBP and his willingness to drive the ball to all fields. After not homering in 105 at-bats in the 2018 season, Adams left the yard eight times as a 19-year-old—most of it spent in the pitcher's paradise of the Midwest League—flashing the power potential to be a middle-of-the-order, run producing bat. His defense and baserunning set a high floor, and could immediately add value to almost any ballclub. The continued progression of his bat-to-ball skills could put him on a fast-track to the big leagues.

Variance: Medium. The tools and athleticism are enticing to project, but Adams has to continue to develop at the plate to make our projection realistic.

Ben Carsley's Fantasy Take: It's always a little worrisome when the utility of the hit tool is the biggest question about a dynasty prospect, but I like the rest of Adams' game too much to be dissuaded from hyping him up here. Besides, even if it does take Adams a while to hit well at the MLB level, his speed and defense should give him a long leash. In short, I really like Adams as a potential speed-based OF3/4 in his prime, even if he gets trapped in more of a fourth outfielder role for the first year or two of his career. He's remains a top-101 dude for me.

─────── ★ ★ ★ *2020 Top 101 Prospect* **#99** ★ ★ ★ ───────

4
D'Shawn Knowles OF OFP: 55   ETA: 2023
Born: 01/16/01   Age: 19   Bats: B   Throws: R   Height: 6'0"   Weight: 165
Origin: International Free Agent, 2017

The Report: Knowles ticks every box for me when it comes to low-low minors bats. He has a loose and lean, athletic frame that should add some good weight, but that eventuality is unlikely to sap his plus-or-better speed or affect his ability to roam in center. Everything's quick twitch, and he already has some feel for routes on the grass. The swing is a bit raw and awkward at times—especially from the right side—but there's plus bat speed and some feel for the barrel to all four quadrants. And even from his weaker side, Knowles can still rip an inside fastball. There's enough underlying athleticism and barrel feel here for me to be…well, not "comfortable," so let's go with "mildly aggressive" in projecting a plus hit tool. The plate approach is also solid given his limited pro experience. Knowles tracks spin all right, and lays off stuff east-west, although he will expand up for the fastball with two strikes.

His swing is geared more for up-the-middle line drives at present, and I don't see a ton of raw power developing long term even as he adds strength over the balance of his teens and early 20s. It might look a bit like 2019 Taylor Trammell in games—as opposed to Taylor Trammell in batting practice—in 2022 or so. And, well, I do like Taylor Trammell. I often say this product isn't a personal pref list, but this is one instance where it is. You could make stronger cases for alternative orders of 4-7 in this system I'm sure, but Knowles is my guy.

Variance: Very high. He's miles from the majors and although the underlying elements of a plus hit tool are there, he hasn't uh, hit much yet.

Ben Carsley's Fantasy Take: Man I love this system. Bret and I sneaked Knowles in at the very end of our top-101 list last season and he justified our faith by holding his own in short-season ball while continuing to display plus tools. Knowles is definitely a slow burn guy, but when in doubt, bet on the plus hit tool. He may lack Adell-ian upside, but Knowles still has all the ingredients of a well-rounded OF3. I'm happy we're somewhat out in front of him.

5. Jeremiah Jackson   SS   OFP: 55   ETA: 2022
Born: 03/26/00   Age: 20   Bats: R   Throws: R   Height: 6'0"   Weight: 165
Origin: Round 2, 2018 Draft (#57 overall)

The Report: The Angels have taken to calibrating their young hitters off an exaggerated hand hitch before introducing the lower half and hinge as their short-season schedule progresses, and Jackson struggled at times to find pitches or consistent fluidity in his swing as he worked through those adjustments. That said, when he did square pitches up they went a long way. He led the Pioneer League in homers thanks to ample lift and twitchy athleticism that lets him whip the barrel through the zone with a good amount of snap. The approach remained highly aggressive, and questionable pitch selection will be an area of needed developmental focus. The defensive future is somewhat in question as well; the jumps and reads off contact remain fairly raw at short, although there is plenty of pure athleticism and arm strength to allow him to keep developing there. The raw foot speed is solid-average and should hold as he continues to fill out a projectable frame.

Variance: High. The ceiling is exciting, but everything is still very raw, especially the hit tool. It will help our confidence in his OFP projection if the mechanics smooth out and the approach starts to show signs of needed progress next season.

Ben Carsley's Fantasy Take: If I had to pick between rolling the dice on one of the Angels' young shortstops, I'd take Jackson over Wilson without much thought. His floor might be a lot lower, sure, but he's also got a Didi Gregorius-esque upside as a power-first shortstop who does enough of everything else to fight for top-10 SS finishes. We're a long ways away from such a future of course, and unlike Gregorius, Jackson isn't a lock to stick at shortstop. But you don't have to squint *too* hard to see a really solid fantasy asset here.

6. Patrick Sandoval LHP   OFP: 55   ETA: 2019
Born: 10/18/96 Age: 23 Bats: L Throws: L Height: 6'3" Weight: 190
Origin: Round 11, 2015 Draft (#319 overall)

The Report: The Triple-A super ball combined with some ongoing command issues that carried over into a bumpy-at-times major league debut to obscure some positive developments in Sandoval's game. Most notably he refined his changeup, and the pitch played really well against hitters at all levels. A long lefty with a high slot, he's always been able to spin the ball pretty well, and the curve continued to miss bats effectively in 2019, while an occasional slider offered serviceable utility. The fastball is a limiting factor, however, with below-average movement and wandering command that too often resulted in fat pitches on a liftable plane. There's enough in the secondary arsenal here to hold out hope for a starting role, at least a nouveau-back-end one who takes you through an order one to two times, but Sandoval will need additional refinement with the hard stuff to get there. Barring a significant overhaul of the Angels depth chart this winter, he should enter the season comfortably in the mix for early-season starts.

Variance: Medium. He's big-league ready and has the tools to compile solid innings and provide 25-man value in the coming season.

Ben Carsley's Fantasy Take: Well, Sandoval isn't very exciting, but at least he's ready to contribute now. I'd worry less about his dynasty value and more about his ability to provide you with some quality innings now if you're in a very deep league. But again, you should be able to replace Sandoval's production with a bunch of dudes on waivers, so don't hesitate to drop him if a more exciting option comes your way or if you're rebuilding.

7. Kyren Paris SS   OFP: 50   ETA: ??
Born: 11/11/01 Age: 18 Bats: R Throws: R Height: 6'0" Weight: 165
Origin: Round 2, 2019 Draft (#55 overall)

The Report: The Angels plucked Paris 55th overall last summer and signed him to a marginally over-slot deal to buy him out of a Cal commitment. He's extremely young, and the physicality remains quite raw, with happy feet at short and an unorthodox swing that doesn't really engage his lower half yet. The athleticism and projection are both notable, however, and he shows outstanding quickness and strong agility on the dirt. The throwing motion is higher-effort, but there's solid velocity already and he should grow into enough to keep him on the left side of the infield.

Paris shows an advanced and patient approach at the plate, and quick wrists help him spray the ball line to line. There's very little ability at present to drive anything with loft, though expected physical gains should result in at least some raw power developing down the line. It's a sum-of-parts profile with value tied to his ability to actualize his physical tools at the six.

Los Angeles Angels 2020

Variance: Extreme. Paris was one of the youngest players selected in last summer's draft, and he logged all of 10 plate appearances in the AZL after signing. The package remains highly theoretical at this point, with a significant gap between present and future physicality.

Ben Carsley's Fantasy Take: A total lottery ticket, but one where the payout is like $50 instead of just $2, at least. Honestly, Paris is the type of way-too-far-away, uber-risky prospect who I think is overvalued in dynasty leagues at present, but if you like him in particular for any reason, you need to get in soon. Such is life in dynasty leagues in 2019.

8. Jose Soriano   RHP   OFP: 50   ETA: 2021/22
Born: 10/20/98   Age: 21   Bats: R   Throws: R   Height: 6'3"   Weight: 168
Origin: International Free Agent, 2016

The Report: Soriano's big boy body has started to grind into being, as his thicker lower and middle sections have filled out considerably and his shoulders have started to carry some adult muscle. He remains somewhat floppy in his movements, though, and has a ways to go in growing into comfort with, and command of, the frame. The delivery's cadence is correspondingly raw, with a noticeably quickened, up-tempo motion producing inconsistent timing and release points that lead to wandering command. The raw stuff is impressive: a mid-90s fastball with some life and finish, combined with a sharp upper-70s curve and signs of changeup utility. The arm is pretty free and easy, and there's some elastic athleticism that lends hope that he can eventually shape it all into a workable starter's mix with enough command. And if he can't, a synced, mature fastball should be able to climb to the top of the double digits and play nicely with an equally amped hook out of the pen.

Variance: High. There's a long path ahead and a lot of maturation to come. The OFP remains firmly in the theoretical stage of things.

Ben Carsley's Fantasy Take: I feel personally attacked by the first two sentences of Soriano's writeup. Unfortunately, the rest doesn't move the needle for me much in terms of dynasty value.

9. Orlando Martinez   SS   OFP: 50   ETA: 2021
Born: 02/17/98   Age: 22   Bats: L   Throws: L   Height: 6'0"   Weight: 185
Origin: International Free Agent, 2017

The Report: The 21-year-old Cuban outfielder missed seven weeks due to injury this season, but still managed to put up 47 extra-base hits in his 88 games played. The 6-foot, 185-pound Martinez is an above-average athlete with good body control and a solid physique. Offensively, he utilizes a gap-to-gap approach and generates a high rate of hard contact. There's some pop in the bat, primarily to right-center field, although he did take top left-handed pitching prospect MacKenzie Gore deep to the opposite field earlier this season. Martinez runs well and is capable of stealing a base, but is not a prolific thief. His advanced baseball instincts and feel for the game ensure astute defensive reads, efficient routes to the ball, and an accurate throwing arm, making him a good defender at all three outfield positions. Martinez is an all-around ballplayer, capable of contributing to the team in a variety of ways. He could be an everyday player, or a valuable fourth outfielder/pinch hitter off the bench.

Variance: Medium. Martinez's defensive versatility and all-around game should allow him to contribute to most ball clubs. It may not be easy to find a starting role initially, especially in a crowded outfield, but the quality of Martinez's contributions should warrant a spot on most rosters, and there's potential for a major-league regular with opportunity.

Ben Carsley's Fantasy Take: Martinez is worth keeping an eye on as he climbs the MiLB ladder, but given the borderline fourth OF profile and how much organizational talent sits in front of him in Orange County, he's best left on watch lists for now.

10. Oliver Ortega RHP
OFP: 50 ETA: 2021
Born: 10/02/96 Age: 23 Bats: R Throws: R Height: 6'0" Weight: 165
Origin: International Free Agent, 2015

Signed by the Angels in 2015, the 6-foot tall, 165-pound Dominican is a quick-twitch athlete with a live right-arm and a max-effort delivery. Ortega pitches confidently, attacking the zone with a power mid-90s fastball, an 11-5 power curveball either side of 80, and a seldom-used but effective low-to-mid-80s changeup. Ortega racked up 121 strikeouts while registering a 3.34 ERA in 94 1/3 innings in the Cal League in 2019. Control can be an issue for the right-hander, as his 49 walks issued detracted from his sparkling .198 opponents batting average. Armed with a power repertoire that can be utilized as a starter, middle reliever, or as a high-leverage fireman, Ortega should be able to work his way to the big leagues if he can command his potent offerings more consistently.

The Next Ten

11. Jahmai Jones 2B
Born: 08/04/97 Age: 22 Bats: R Throws: R Height: 5'11" Weight: 205
Origin: Round 2, 2015 Draft (#70 overall)

It was a tough year for Jones, who struggled to produce or advance his skills in a full-season stint at Double-A. He remains an impressive pure athlete with strength and some quick-burst into fluid movement patterns, but none of it has really translated to baseball skills as of yet in spite of a renowned work ethic. The organization has fiddled with his swing several times, but the most recent fruits of those labors have all been stiff and lacking for the kind of quickness or plane to juice his all-too-rare barrelled balls. The approach is okay, but the hit tool remains lagging and he struggles to maximize bat speed or attack hittable pitches the way he needs to. His play at the keystone hasn't progressed as hoped, either, with actions that haven't yet morphed into more natural or nuanced play. Jones still deserves a "he's only 22" pass on some of this, but the lack of progress in refining it all into a coherent MLB-quality package at this point is starting to get concerning.

12 Trent Deveaux   OF
Born: 05/04/00   Age: 20   Bats: R   Throws: R   Height: 6'0"   Weight: 160
Origin: International Free Agent, 2017

This list is peppered with high-end athletes and Deveaux might be the best of the lot. The frame reminds me of high school Jo Adell and he was an Olympic-caliber sprinter prospect in the Bahamas. It's a body to dream on and there's some bat speed here as well. But if you thought Jeremiah Jackson had an exaggerated hitch, well, Deveaux has to churn an entire crock of creamery butter during his hand path. It's a long load, and it often leaves him late on hard stuff that isn't center cut and he's unable to adjust to offspeed. The overall baseball profile is rawer than Jackson and Knowles too, and the speed plays down in the outfield at present. The bat control isn't hopeless despite the multiple exaggerated timing mechanisms—there's a Jo Adellish leg kick in the mix too—so I'm going to give Deveaux a long leash as we are entering the part of this list that lacks much in the way of upside. But the low end of the extreme variance here is "never gets out of A-ball."

13 Leonardo Rivas   SS
Born: 10/10/97   Age: 22   Bats: B   Throws: R   Height: 5'10"   Weight: 150
Origin: International Free Agent, 2014

Listed at 5-foot-10 and 150 pounds, the 22-year-old infielder doesn't possess much power, but that appears to be Rivas' only weakness in an otherwise solid all-around skill set. A strong arm, soft hands, and good range make him a potential plus defender in the middle of the infield, and he was also impressive in nine starts in center field this season, adding defensive versatility to his resume. The switch-hitting infielder from Venezuela was limited to 73 games due to injury, but managed to post an average offensive effort while young for High-A.

For the second consecutive season, Rivas has performed drastically differently from each side of the plate. Whereas the right-handed swing is quick and compact, he whiffs on far too many pitches in the zone from the other side of the plate. As skilled as Rivas is defensively, hitting from the right side full-time may help focus that development and expedite his progress toward the major leagues.

14 Jared Walsh   1B/LHP
Born: 07/30/93   Age: 26   Bats: L   Throws: L   Height: 6'0"   Weight: 210
Origin: Round 39, 2015 Draft (#1185 overall)

Walsh plays both ways, baby, and he rode that two-way street right on up to the big leagues last year, which already constitutes an 80-grade effort for a guy drafted 1,185th overall. Walsh's strength and plus raw power have been interesting for a while now, particularly once he started bringing it into games against better competition in 2018. He continued the power onslaught with the goofy ball at Triple-A last year, though major league arms ate his lunch across his sporadic at-bats against the best of the best. The swing is fluid in spite of stiffness, but a deficit of bat speed fed his destruction by premium velocity in The Show. Given time to adjust, there's enough baseline of bat-to-ball and approach to warrant controlled optimism that he can hit some dingers while offering first base/corner outfield versatility.

That's mildly interesting on its own but he also just so happens to spin it pretty good off the bump. His hook plays well off a low-90s fastball that features quality sink from the left side. He's still expectedly raw as far as mechanical consistency goes, though the delivery is simple enough that he retains some command projection. If he hits enough to offer bench depth on that side of the ball there's a nice little bit of value to be found in his 26th-man profile.

15 Chris Rodriguez   RHP
Born: 07/20/98   Age: 21   Bats: R   Throws: R   Height: 6'2"   Weight: 185
Origin: Round 4, 2016 Draft (#126 overall)

The Floridian fireballer was drafted out of high school by the Angels in the fourth round of the 2016 Draft, and after showing an intriguing four-pitch mix in the low minors he missed the entire 2018 season with a back injury. The 20-year-old made his 2019 debut at Inland Empire and again showcased the same electric four-pitch arsenal seemingly no worse for the wear. The stuff is headlined by a mid-90s heater that moves well in two directions. He also throws a nasty, hard slider, along with both a changeup in the mid 80s and a solid 11-to-5 curveball that'll both flash as above-average offerings. In three Cal League appearances Rodriguez whiffed a bunch of guys and stayed off barrels effectively, but unfortunately his back issues resurfaced and the young righty underwent a procedure that prematurely ended his 2019 campaign. Rodriguez's talent is apparent, as he's demonstrated big-league ability when healthy enough to take the mound. The Angels will certainly hope to get him back on the field and working again towards that OFP in 2020.

16 Luis Madero   RHP
Born: 04/15/97   Age: 23   Bats: R   Throws: R   Height: 6'3"   Weight: 185
Origin: International Free Agent, 2013

The 22-year-old Venezuelan began the 2019 season in the California League but needed just four appearances to earn a promotion to Double-A. The 6-foot-3 Madero pairs quick-twitch athleticism with a low-three-quarters arm slot, attacking hitters with a 92-93 mph fastball, a slurvy 80 mph breaking ball that darts across the strike zone, and a developing mid-80s changeup. His delivery, which includes a waist-high leg kick, can get long, and that leads to occasionally inconsistent command. After posting a 3.79 ERA and limiting opponents to a .253 batting average in his initial 40 1/3 Southern League innings pitched, hitters figured him out in the second half and the performance hit a wall. The righty's three-pitch attack may ultimately be best suited for the bullpen, where his versatility and durability could allow him to pitch multiple innings per appearance and contribute valuable depth across a 162-game season.

17 Hector Yan   LHP
Born: 04/26/99   Age: 21   Bats: L   Throws: L   Height: 5'11"   Weight: 180
Origin: International Free Agent, 2015

Signed out of the Dominican in 2015, Yan made his full-season debut at Burlington and promptly led the Midwest League in K% as one of the younger arms in the league. Unfortunately, he also came close to leading the circuit in walk rate, and that's where our plot thickens. A shorter, physically maxed southpaw, Yan's raw stuff is highly intriguing: a mid-90s fastball that'll top at 97, a biting slider that can take hitters out of the zone, and a hard splitter that offers utility as a second chase pitch. To get the stuff to play against better hitters, however, he'll have to overcome an unorthodox delivery with a low, sweeping leg kick and extreme crossfire; neither the control nor command currently project to approach average. The stuff is good enough that with standard refinement he can get very good hitters out, but absent a jump in command projection a useful if frustrating middle relief track is the one he's on.

18 Nathan Bates   RHP
Born: 03/01/94   Age: 26   Bats: R   Throws: R   Height: 6'6"   Weight: 205
Origin: Round 15, 2015 Draft (#465 overall)

The 6-foot-6 right-hander has the look of a major leaguer when he toes the rubber and fires his mid-90s fastball and hard curve from a high three-quarters slot. The "when he toes the rubber" part is the lede, however; Bates has been limited to just 108 1/3 innings in the five years since the Angels popped him in the 15th round on account of both injury and suspension. He looked good in eight late-season appearances for Inland Empire in 2019, and if he can stay healthy and on the field going forward, the hard-throwing Bates could become a valuable one- or two-inning reliever out of the bullpen.

19 Livan Soto   SS
Born: 06/22/00   Age: 20   Bats: L   Throws: R   Height: 6'0"   Weight: 160
Origin: International Free Agent, 2017

One of the prospects caught up in the Braves' international signing scandal a few years back, Soto signed a contract with Anaheim for $850k two winters ago and made his way to the Midwest League this year on the back of a solid defensive starter kit at the six. The arm is plenty for the left side, and his lateral movement is the low and quick kind that lends to quality range. He's started filling out his 6-foot frame, but rounded shoulders don't suggest a ton of brute strength development is forthcoming, and there is no power at all in the offensive game. A quick load and flat bat at launch produce minimal plane on his swings, though he has shown quality strike zone awareness and his quick stroke produces a lot of contact. There are some pieces to build with here, though he lacks sufficient straight-line speed to make the offensive profile work as a slap-and-dasher.

20 Michael Hermosillo OF
Born: 01/17/95   Age: 25   Bats: R   Throws: R   Height: 6'0"   Weight: 205
Origin: Round 28, 2013 Draft (#847 overall)

So it's going to be hard to finagle playing time in the Angels outfield in the coming years. Hermosillo has struggled to capitalize on his 2017 breakout year, dealing with injuries the past two seasons. His recovery from sports hernia surgery cost him the first two months of 2019, and while he's continued to hit in Triple-A, his brief MLB cameos haven't gone well. The hit tool was the big question as a prospect, and Hermosillo has struggled with offspeed in the majors and can't always catch up to better velocity. He's strong enough to do damage when he does connect and is a plus runner that can handle all three outfield spots, so if he refines some stuff with more MLB reps, there's a perfectly fine bench outfielder here. It's going to be tough to get those reps, although I suppose even Mike Trout needs a day off now and again.

Personal Cheeseball

PC Gareth Morgan OF
Born: 04/12/96   Age: 24   Bats: R   Throws: R   Height: 6'4"   Weight: 265
Origin: Round 2, 2014 Draft (#74 overall)

Morgan's displays of immense raw power as a Canadian prep enamored the Mariners enough to select him with the 74th-overall pick in the 2014 Draft. After struggling to develop offensively, including striking out 180+ times in the 2017 and 2018 seasons, the Mariners released Morgan eight games into the 2019 season. The Angels quickly signed him and sent him to their own Cal League affiliate in Inland Empire, where the change of scenery energized Morgan into a power surge as he hit .290 with 20 home runs in his first 44 games in the Angels organization. After earning a promotion to Double-A, the advanced pitching stymied the big fella, as he homered only once while striking out 55 times in 27 games at the higher level. Listed at 6-foot-4 and 265 pounds, Morgan is somewhat shockingly mobile on the basepaths and even demonstrates okay athleticism in the outfield (he managed to log 11 games of center field reps this season). Although he's adequate in the field, this is a brawny, old school DHing slugger profile. With continued development of his bat-to-ball abilities, Morgan could be a fun power bat with a best-case scenario looking not unlike Franmil Reyes.

Low Minors Sleeper

LMS **Alexander Ramirez   OF**
Born: 08/29/02   Age: 17   Bats: R   Throws: R   Height: 6'2"   Weight: 180
Origin: International Free Agent, 2018

Ramirez was a seven-figure J2 signing as one of the younger high-end prospects in the 2018 IFA class, and at the time of his signing listed out at 6-foot-1 and 180 pounds. That's as a 16-year-old, born in the second half of 2002. The body is obscenely projectable, and there's a whole bunch of present strength already to build on. He shows a quiet, balanced swing from the right side with outstanding extension and plane to drive pitches. It's a prototypical power-hitting corner outfield profile, and after he logged 39 games in the DSL last season it'll be interesting to see how aggressive the club gets as far as potentially bringing him stateside in 2020. He is approximately 4.3 light years away from making a Major League roster if it all comes together, but there's a non-zero chance he grows into a physical monster and destroys worlds one day.

Top Talents 25 and Under (as of 4/1/2020)

1. Shohei Ohtani
2. Jo Adell
3. Griffin Canning
4. Brandon Marsh
5. Jordyn Adams
6. David Fletcher
7. D'Shawn Knowles
8. Matt Thaiss
9. José Suarez
10. Jeremiah Jackson

Was there some concern that Adell evangelist (Adellvangelist? Quick, take it before Adele does) Craig Goldstein would summarily fire me when I submitted this list with Ohtani at the perch? No, not at all! Silly you'd even ask. Ridiculous, really...

As to why Ohtani ranks first, I would point dually to his present body of work and the potential he retains to be so much more. As a first-season NPB import and 23-year-old, Ohtani was 22 percent better than league average with the bat and 23 percent from the mound. He was called a "high school hitter" that spring training and then proceeded to win Rookie of the Year with his bat when his arm gave out—an arm that comes easy 97 plus and got 63 punchouts in 50 2/3 innings. Last season held regression at the plate, yes, but Ohtani also spent the entire campaign in grueling rehabilitation from Tommy John surgery, a surgery whose effects on batters is underappreciated. We've seen quite a lot from Ohtani, but there's ample reason to believe the best is yet to come.

Canning was 22 when he debuted and was more okay-good than good-great, but he was nevertheless basically the ace of an Angels rotation that depressed in multiple ways. The major concern that caused the second-round draft pick to fall to California/Anaheim/Los Angeles was durability, and though he was shut down in August with elbow inflammation, it's still looking like the UCLA product will live up to his mid-rotation potential.

Fletcher is one of those diminutive infielders who seems destined to be underrated; his six home runs in 653 plate appearances were both the league's second-worst rate (only Yolmer Sánchez had fewer home runs per at-bat among qualified players) and, given the rocket ball, likely near the limit of his output. He still managed to be a league-average batter thanks to 30 doubles, a three percent hike in walk rate (to an acceptable eight percent), and a dip in strikeout rate (from 11 to 10 percent). Combined with positional versatility, Fletch has proved himself a valuable piece.

The Angels raised eyebrows in 2016 when they selected defensively marginal catcher Thaiss with the 16th overall pick, and got them up into "you're going to give yourself wrinkles" territory when they immediately shifted him to first and tagged him with a host of other issues to overcome. Blocked by Albert Pujols, Thaiss now needs to prove he can handle the hot corner, and likely also bat a bit better than his 91 DRC+ last season, but it's not hard to see him quickly developing into a plus platoon/bench piece or average regular.

Suarez is difficult to rank here, being that he was one of MLB's worst starters last season. Ranking a pitcher who posted nearly negative three wins and a DRA 84 percent worse than average might seem both optimistic and an indictment of the Angels' system, but several caveats are useful. Suarez pitched the entire season at 21, almost certainly would have spent more time developing in the minors had not circumstance conscripted him, and simply cannot surrender 2.6 homers per nine again. The only place to go is up, there's just a ways to climb. Which feels like a metaphor for some team…

Part 3: Featured Articles

The Baseball Is Juiced (Again)

Robert Arthur

This article originally appeared at Baseball Prospectus on April 5, 2019.

It started when the normally reliable Chris Sale got lit up for three homers by the Mariners in the Red Sox's season opener. It was part of a record number of taters that flew on Opening Day, as starters from Sale to Zack Greinke were taken deep by the handful. Then Christian Yelich hit a home run in each of his first four games, tying yet another MLB record, this one for consecutive games with a dinger to start a season.

It didn't take long for fans and players to begin whispering and tweeting about the baseballs being juiced again. It's early yet for us to come to any definitive conclusion about the 2019 season, but preliminary data shows that the baseball has returned to its aerodynamic peak. Whether that means this season will smash home run records like 2017 did remains to be seen.

Before home run explosion over the last few years, no one worried too much about the baseball's air resistance. While MLB and Rawlings (the company that manufactures the official baseballs) kept track of dozens of metrics to make sure that the ball was consistent from month to month, they didn't measure drag.

But drag is incredibly important in determining how likely a hitter is to knock one out of the park. As baseballs become more aerodynamic, they travel further given a certain initial velocity. A deep fly ball that might have been caught at the warning track can instead go into the first row of the stands. A three percent change in drag coefficient can work to add about five feet to a well-hit fly ball, which can in turn increase home runs league wide by an astounding 10-15 percent.

It's possible to measure the aerodynamics of the baseball using the pitch-tracking radars currently in place in each MLB ballpark. By calculating the loss of speed from when the pitch is released to when it crosses the plate, you can directly measure the drag coefficient on the baseball. I first wrote about the role of decreasing drag in boosting home runs in 2017, and MLB's commission of scientists and statisticians later confirmed that the more aerodynamic baseballs

Los Angeles Angels 2020

in use that year were largely to blame for the spike in home runs. The same commission rejected some alternate hypotheses, like rising temperatures and a league-wide boost in launch angle pushing more balls over the fence.

The current era has featured some large fluctuations in drag coefficient, leading to first an explosion in 2016 and 2017, and then a dialing back of homers last year. Curious about the record-breaking home run tallies in the last few days, I used the same methodology to measure the aerodynamics of the baseballs so far in 2019.

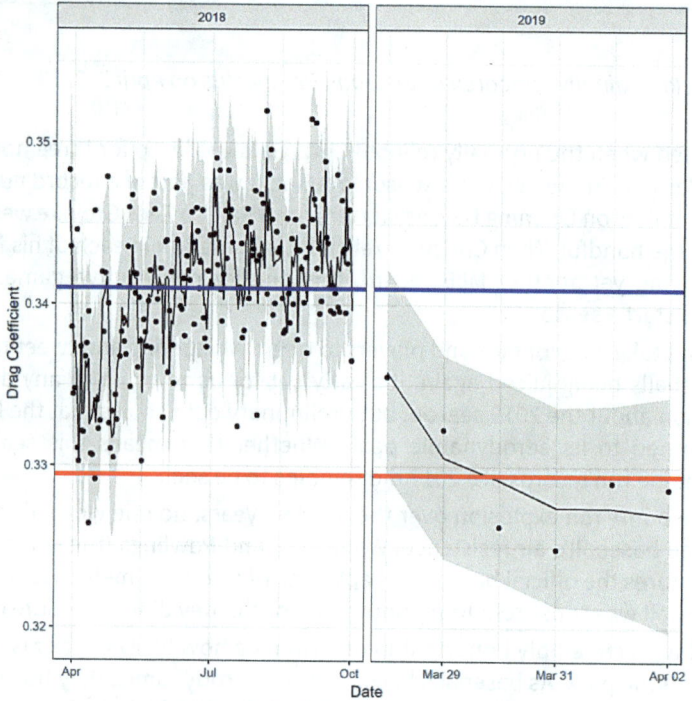

We're only a week into the 2019 season, but the drag numbers so far are among the lowest recorded in the last calendar year. With apologies for gory math, the current 2019 season average drag coefficient (the red line) would be below the 95 percent credible interval (the shaded area) for about nine-tenths of the 2018 season. (I used a Bayesian Random Walk model implemented in INLA to calculate these credible intervals, averaging the drag numbers in each game and adjusting for park.)

There were only a handful of six-day stretches in 2018 that had drag numbers below what we're seeing now, and most were in late June and early July. All of this means that 2019's data so far is quite a bit different than what we saw through most of last year.

These drag coefficients factor out the effects of temperature and air density, so they aren't a product of April cold. However, the numbers could be deceptive if the radars used to track pitches have changed from year to year. I consulted with some experts within baseball who were not aware of any specific modifications to the radar this year that could produce this pattern, but it's an important caveat of which to be aware.

On the one hand, it's only been six days, and we don't quite have the statistical basis to say that these drag coefficients are unprecedented compared to 2018. On the other hand, we've witnessed about 5,000 fastballs so far this season, so it's not as if our sample size is small. At least so far, the baseball has played like it's much more aerodynamic than it was last year. In fact, the current drag coefficient is really only comparable to 2017, when the baseballs were more aerodynamic than they had been in at least a decade.

It's not just fancy radar tracking indicating that the baseball is flying through the air more easily. The current number of home runs per game (as of this writing) is the highest it's been since the heady days of 2017, the year that teams and players broke dinger-related records everywhere you looked. That's especially remarkable considering that we're in what is typically the coldest part of the regular season, when lower temperatures and higher winds tend to suppress offense and keep balls in the air within the park. Comparing only from April to April, this year's rate of home runs per fly ball is even a little bit higher than it was in 2017.

With that said, the current measurements are no guarantee that 2019 will be another year of record-shattering homer hitting. The trouble with the drag measurements is that they are not consistent from June to August, from week to week, or even sometimes from day to day. Whether because of natural manufacturing variation or differences in the underlying supplies of cowhide and thread that go into the baseballs, drag has a tendency to fluctuate up and down over the course of a year. So the homers that fly in the first week of April wouldn't necessarily clear the fence a week later.

It's possible that this one-week drop in drag coefficient subsides and the baseball returns to its 2018 levels. On the other hand, it's almost equally probable that the ball becomes even more slippery and flies ever farther. Either way, it's clear that the baseball's air resistance is something to keep an eye on for the remainder of the 2019 season.

—*Robert Arthur is an author of Baseball Prospectus.*

The Moral Hazard of Playing It Safe

Craig Goldstein

This article originally appeared at Baseball Prospectus on August 6, 2019.

A couple days prior to the trade deadline, amidst a sea of tranquility posing as the lead up to the trade deadline, Bob Nightengale took to Twitter. Nightengale, who was probably wearing his pants backwards at the time, tweeted that MLB GMs were coming around on the idea that the unified trade deadline should be moved back from July 31 to August 15, so they could better assess their positions in the standings and whether they should buy or sell. To which I said:

This might strike some as reductive and churlish. And it might be that, but it isn't really wrong, either. Jeff Quinton wrote a great piece discussing the environmental factors that enable front offices to avoid risk without upsetting the apple cart within their own fanbases. I don't believe that it goes far enough, however. His article gives us the proper framework through which to understand why these behaviors have been allowed to seep into front offices throughout the league. Understanding the reasons behind these actions are different from excusing them, though, and GMs should not be let off the hook for their non-competitive approach to the trade deadline (much less the offseason).

⚾   ⚾   ⚾

It's fair to say that fans as a group have rarely, if ever, been pro-player. It is also fair to say that in the time during and following the Moneyball revolution, the pendulum swung from fans who cared intensely about winning in the moment (and thus might be intolerant of a rebuilding approach) to fans who supported building a team that could compete throughout multiple seasons, viewing the playoffs as a crapshoot, with the thought that getting multiple bites at the apple was a better approach than taking a bigger bite in any one season.

There's nothing wrong with that approach, and I still find merit in that argument. However, it seems that the pendulum has swung too far in that direction. Teams are overvaluing some of the individual factors that make themselves long-term contenders rather than attempting to seize a championship when given the opportunity. It's a difficult needle to thread.

And surely, they (and those in similar positions) would have liked another two weeks to clarify where they stand so as to better marshal their resources. We've all asked for a few more minutes when staring at a menu. But all of these GMs and front office personnel are where they are to make difficult decisions. They have proprietary data and internal analysts dedicated to understanding their position relative to the rest of the league, and how any move in the here and now impacts their long-term vision. To complain (if that report is accurate) that over half the season is not enough to properly assess their season is bullshit of the highest order. Move the deadline, and you'd simply have increasingly discounted trade offers because teams would be acquiring even less control of anyone they're acquiring, rental or not.

Major league front offices are behaving like the managers they lampooned two decades ago. They're effectively sacrificing a runner to second in the ninth inning—not because it's the correct move, but rather because it is safe. It used to be that the phrase "moral hazard" was used to describe general managers who made ill-fated, short-sighted decisions aimed at locking in wins and securing their jobs at the expense of their team's future. Now, general managers are guilty of committing moral hazards in the opposite direction, playing it utterly safe and terrified of becoming scapegoats.

In lieu of bold action, they opt to pussyfoot around a current window of contention, choosing instead to play the long game and stack up years of control like they're blocks in a game of Jenga. GMs pass on signing quality players in free agency because the back-end of the deal might look bad, and because they might be able to squeeze out 70 percent of the production from a player who costs a tenth as much. That's a safer investment, too, because it's also hard to prove a negative—it's impossible to prove that Manny Machado would make the Mets a playoff team in 2019-2020, but it's easy to say that the back half of Robinson Cano's contract sucks. Owners, who rule over GM's jobs, are also humans with human brain processes that will always make the so-called albatross contract uglier than the road not taken.

These days, GMs are remembered for the bad deals they make and the surplus value they generate, not the acquisition of expensive, necessary talents that meet their market worth (or fall slightly short while still providing significant on-field value). And front offices know that one or two expensive misfires can cost them their jobs, no matter how many good deals they make.

No front office exemplifies this ethos more than the Toronto Blue Jays. General Manager Ross Atkins had this to say following the Blue Jays underwhelming trade deadline:

This is by no means the first time that an executive will cite years of control to justify their actions, which is often just another way of saying "don't look at what we got, look at how much we got of it." Atkins touts quantity to elide the discussion of quality—either, that of the players acquired, or those given up. Remember: the other teams presumably value years of control, too.

Atkins also had some thoughts to offer regarding free agents back in early 2018:

Los Angeles Angels 2020

This ignores, of course, whether the player can create enough value in the front end of a contract to justify the longer term of a deal, and the decline that often occurs in the back end. It also ignores whether the player can fill a need the team requires and put them in a position to compete for and win a championship. But as teams seemingly avoid contention at all, where they might end up having to consider and later justify some of these tough decisions, we still see risk-averse approaches.

Anthony Fenech's article on two trades that recently extended GM Al Avila didn't make got at this issue rather well:

> Passing on those deals was defensible: Both players had yet to break out and trading [Michael] Fulmer—a pitcher who appeared to be a future ace, no matter his injury concerns—would have taken serious gumption, opening Avila up to strong criticism.

Avoiding strong criticism is something each of us can understand as a motivation, but the avoidance of criticism only matters if that criticism is valid. In Fulmer's case, shoving his injury concerns aside affects not only the years that the team controls him (he is currently missing a full season due to Tommy John surgery) but also the quality of those seasons, as his knee and elbow injuries combined to dampen his effectiveness even when healthy enough to pitch. But it was easy to present the then-current image of Fulmer as a top of the rotation pitcher who the team had under its domain for the next five seasons as something to build around. The status quo isn't nearly as often second-guessed as a decision that disrupts it.

⚾ ⚾ ⚾

MLB GMs are risk-averse to a fault. They are ivy-educated and consulting firm-approved, and yet they can't seem to avoid leaving wins on the table in their all-consuming lust for a non-existent $/WAR championship. They are supposed to zig when everyone else zags, and not merely pay lip service to the idea of zigging through a calculated PR plan built on convincing the fan base their approach is novel when it actually apes most of their competitors. Instead they've become far more concerned with making safe, accepted-by-the-new-common-wisdom decisions, such that our prior understanding of what a moral hazard is has become inverted.

I can't blame them entirely, and not only because of the reasons that Quinton illuminated in his article, but also because of the damage wrought by the introduction of the second wild card (WC2) spot. MLB's desire to have more teams in playoff contention has sparked anti-competitive behavior. Teams know now that they do not need to swing big as they assemble their roster because there is a good chance that a mediocre team can either catch fire and capture a division, or muddle along until they back into the WC2.

Simultaneously, the one-game playoff has neutered the WC1, putting an entire season on the flip of a coin like some sort of baseball-obsessed Anton Chigurh. While the one-game playoff makes sense as a way to increase the value of winning a division, it also means that if a front office doesn't like its chances of overcoming a behemoth like the Dodgers or Astros in the offseason, they have few incentives to chase glory. Similarly, the relative inaction in the NL Central at the trade deadline—despite a wide open division—can be explained by the idea that any high-variance investment could still result in only a wild card (or worse) result, given the mere two months left in the season to make an impact.

⚾ ⚾ ⚾

As stated at the top, we should not confuse reasons for excuses. The implementation of the second wild card is just one of many environmental factors that influence how each front office operates. I am convinced that it is one of the larger factors, but I am also convinced that organizations need to shed the yoke of "efficiency at all costs" so that they can instead pursue competition, as the spirit of the game intends. Until they do, we're all deadline losers.

—*Craig Goldstein is an author of Baseball Prospectus.*

Index of Names

Adams, Jordyn 87, 108	Keller, Kyle 103
Adell, Jo 88, 107	Kelly, Ty 93
Anderson, Justin 46	Knowles, D'Shawn 94, 109
Andriese, Matt 48	La Stella, Tommy 28
Aquino, Stiward 103	Madero, Luis 103, 115
Bard, Luke 50	Maitan, Kevin 95
Barnes, Jacob 52	Markel, Parker 103
Barria, Jaime 54	Marsh, Brandon 96, 108
Bates, Nathan 116	Martinez, Orlando 101, 112
Bedrosian, Cam 56	Mattson, Isaac 103
Bemboom, Anthony 89	Mayers, Mike 103
Bour, Justin 18	Middleton, Keynan 99
Bradish, Kyle 103	Morgan, Gareth 117
Bundy, Dylan 58	Ohtani, Shohei 97, 100
Buttrey, Ty 60	Ortega, Oliver 113
Cahill, Trevor 62	Paris, Kyren 111
Canning, Griffin 64	Peña, Félix 72
Castillo, Jesus 103	Peters, Dillon 70
Castro, Jason 20	Pujols, Albert 30
Cole, Taylor 66	Ramirez, Alexander 118
Cowart, Kaleb 101	Ramirez, JC 103
Deveaux, Trent 90, 114	Ramirez, Neil 103
English, William 103	Ramirez, Noé 74
Fletcher, David 22	Rendon, Anthony 32
Goodwin, Brian 24	Rengifo, Luis 34
Heaney, Andrew 68	Rivas, Leonardo 114
Hermosillo, Michael 26, 117	Robles, Hansel 76
Hernandez, Aaron 103	Rodriguez, Chris 103, 115
Jackson, Jeremiah 91, 110	Rodriguez, Jose 103
Jewell, Jake 103	Rondon, Adrian 101
Jones, Jahmai 92, 113	Sandoval, Patrick 79, 111

Los Angeles Angels 2020

Simmons, Andrelton 36
Skaggs, Tyler 81
Soriano, Jose 103, 112
Soto, Livan 101, 116
Stassi, Max 38
Suarez, Jose 83
Teheran, Julio 85
Thaiss, Matt 40
Tovar, Wilfredo 101
Trout, Mike 42
Upton, Justin 44
Walsh, Jared 98, 114
Ward, Taylor 101
Yan, Hector 103, 116